NATURE HAS FLAVOR

LIRON MELLER

Cooking Your Way to a Healthier Life

Nature Has Flavor: Cooking your Way to a Healthier Life

© Become Healthier Inc. 2016

All Rights Reserved. No part of this book may be reproduced or utilized in any form or by any means, electronic or mechanical, including photocopying, recording, or by any information storage and retrieval system, without permission in writing from the publisher. For information, contact Liron Meller at Info@NatureHasFlavor.com.

Library of Congress Control Number: 2016949086

ISBN: 978-0-9978622-1-8 (Print)

ISBN: 978-0-9978622-0-1 (E-book)

Nature Has Flavor: Cooking your Way to a Healthier Life / Liron Meller

Author: Liron Meller
Recipe Development: Liron Meller
Editor: Danny Horgan
Book Design: Kristin Roybal, Pulsebeam.com

Nature Has Flavor is a Become Healthier Inc. company. For more information about Nature Has Flavor, visit NatureHasFlavor.com or call 888.969.CHEF (2433).

Welcome Message from Nature Has Flavor Co-Founder, Liron Meller

Hello, and welcome to the first day of a life-changing new adventure.

My name is Liron Meller, and I'm the co-founder of *Nature Has Flavor*. Since the age of 14, I've worked as a chef in restaurants around the world, constantly honing my craft and developing an ever-growing appreciation of hearty, delicious food.

My journey into the plant-based lifestyle was anything but easy. After years of eating the standard American diet, I found myself with low energy and a slew of health issues, the worst of which was a cancerous tumor on my kidney. Dejected and confused, I knew I had to find out more about why I had become so sick.

So I did my research. I poured through books, medical texts, and scientific studies, trying to get to the root cause of my illnesses. What I found shocked me: **Perhaps more than any other factor, our health is influenced by what we eat.** More specifically, many of the foods we've been taught are necessary for proper nutrition—meat, dairy, fish, and eggs—may be the origin of heart disease, type 2 diabetes, high cholesterol, and more.

As a chef, this information was **not** what I wanted to hear. My career had been spent preparing dishes that included creamy sauces, egg-based textures, and substantial amounts of meat—how could I cook without them? And what about the nutrition information we constantly see in the media? Don't we **need** protein from meat, dairy from calcium, and healthy fats from fish?

My doubts were put to rest when I began the plant-based diet myself. Intrinsically, I had always known vegetables were good for me, but I never knew how amazing I could feel when I made them the basis of my meals. Within months of removing animal products from my diet, my illnesses subsided. I felt decades younger and had more energy than I knew was possible.

But there was still the issue of cooking—how could I express my talents as a chef using only plant-based foods? I began experimenting with my dishes, substituting animal products with plants and developing entirely new recipes. The result? **I learned that the most robust, mouthwatering flavors I could use as a chef all came from nature.** And by using my decades of experience, I could craft nature's gifts into delectable meals for any occasion.

What you will find in this booklet is a 21-day, step-by-step guide for preparing breakfast, lunch, and dinner using only healthy, plant-based foods. What *we* hope to show you at *Nature Has Flavor* is that eating healthy does not mean sacrificing taste. The recipes in this book will keep you excited about your new journey, packing the goodness of nature's flavors into every bite you take. The *Nature Has Flavor* community will also be there to support you, giving you guidance when you feel lost and helping you rebound from any mistakes. More than anything, we are a community dedicated to helping each other through diet, and we acknowledge that slipups are part of the journey to optimal health.

I never would have thought that I would become an advocate of plant-based cooking. But what's even more amazing is that my road to recovery from illness led me back to the area I'm most passionate about—food. I look forward to sharing that passion with you through these recipes.

Liron Meller

Chapter 1

The Western Diet vs. The Plant-Based Diet

If you ever need proof that the standard Western diet **isn't** working, you simply need to look around you.

Americans, as a whole, are not healthy. Despite having unprecedented access to medical treatment, clean water, and ample amounts of healthy foods, we are still bigger and sicker than we've ever been. So what exactly is going on?

The answer lies in what we put into our bodies. The United States food pyramid, created in 1992 by the United States Department of Agriculture (USDA), has long served as our guide to eating a balanced, healthy diet, and it has influenced everything from nutrition textbooks to the food served at public schools and hospitals. But where has it gotten us? If the statistics are any indication, the advice may be doing more harm than good:

- Over 29 million Americans have diabetes, and roughly 86 million American adults have prediabetes. Together, these Americans make up more than 42% of the country's population.[1]

- The average American woman in 2015 weighed 166.2 pounds—almost exactly as much as the average American man (166.3 pounds) in the 1960s.[2]

- The average American man in 2015 tipped the scales at over 195 pounds.

- Every year, some 735,000 Americans have a heart attack, and one in every four American deaths can be attributed to heart disease.[3]

- A whopping 73.5 million American adults have high cholesterol.[4]

Obviously, we're doing something wrong. But are **that** many Americans really guilty of just eating too much junk food? The answer may surprise you.

You see, many of the foods we've long considered "healthy" are anything but good for us. These foods slowly eat away at our kidneys, arteries, and bones, leading to long-term destruction of our health and vitality. What's even more disturbing is that many of these foods are included on the United States food pyramid.

To really examine the damaging effects of everyday foods, let's examine the diet of two typical Americans—a 40-something woman who juggles a career with raising a family and a 40-something man who works over 50 hours a week at a corporate office:

Woman

Morning

After the woman gets her kids ready for school, she has to rush to work, forcing her to stop at a Starbucks for breakfast. She purchases a bagel with cream cheese and a large coffee, which she sweetens with sugar and cream.

Afternoon

Lunch rolls around, and the woman eats a typical "well-rounded" meal, consisting of a turkey sandwich with lettuce and tomato, potato chips, a container of Greek yogurt with added fruit, and a bottle of apple juice.

Just a few hours later, the woman is tired and in need of a snack. She goes to the office vending machine to buy a bag of cheese-filled pretzels. To wash it down, she guzzles another cup of coffee.

Evening

For dinner, the woman—tired from her day and caffeine crashes—decides to microwave frozen meals for herself and her family. Time is at a premium on her busy schedule, and summoning the energy to prepare a fresh meal just doesn't seem possible. On her plate tonight are pork chops, macaroni and cheese, and string beans, which she compliments with a few hash browned potatoes.

It's almost time for bed, and the woman feels she deserves a treat from her long day. She goes into her freezer to grab a pint of chocolate swirl ice cream. She eats half of the container, falls asleep, and then does it all again the next day.

Man

Morning

The man's first meeting is bright and early, so breakfast will be whatever is served at the conference table. On this morning, that means donuts and pastries from a local bakery, along with a limitless stream of coffee. The man polishes off a cheese danish and a donut over the course of the 90-minute meeting and manages to squeeze in three cups of coffee, each mixed with ample amounts of cream and sugar.

Afternoon

Working 50 hours a week means the man has little energy to prepare his own lunches. So he does what most Americans do when they're busy—he relies on fast food. Today's pick is a large BLT from Subway, complemented by a bag of chips, a 20oz bottle of Coke, and a cookie for dessert.

By the time 3:00 rolls around, the man is exhausted and ready for a nap. But he has another meeting he needs to be ready for by 3:30, so he takes a trip to the vending machine to grab a can of Coke and a candy bar. The snack temporarily perks him up, giving him just enough energy to make it through the meeting.

Evening

It's 7:30, and the man is just now finishing his day at work. His co-workers invite him out for drinks, and he accepts the invitation so he can blow off steam. They head out to a local bar.

Because the man hasn't eaten anything since his mid-afternoon candy bar, his body is starving for nutrients. His eyes glance over the bar's menu, and having to choose from limited options, the man decides on a chicken wrap with a side of fries. He eats as he puts away several pints of beer to wind down from the busy day.

The man gets home at 10:30. He finds himself wanting dessert, but his pantries are empty. He settles on a few glasses of orange juice, which at least will give him the sugar rush he's looking for.

If you think the referenced woman and man are making unhealthy food choices, you're right. But amazingly, their diets would meet all food group recommendations on the United States food pyramid. In their eyes, they're doing nothing wrong. Meanwhile, their diets could be causing headaches, low energy, weight gain, and more.

The Plant-Based Alternative

It's clear our current way of eating isn't working. But what can we subtract from the food pyramid without sacrificing our health?

At **Nature Has Flavor**, we believe in making vegetables, fruits, nuts, seeds, whole grains, and legumes the basis of our diet. What you won't find in our meals are any types of animal products, including meat, dairy, eggs, and seafood. Why? Because we believe eating this way allows our bodies to function the way they're **supposed** to—sustainably energetic and free from chronic illness.

There is an overwhelming amount of evidence supporting the use of plant-based diets. Just some of this research includes:

- A number of studies have indicated that plant-based diets may prevent, arrest, and even reverse heart disease [5][6]

- A 2009 study of over 60,000 men and women showed that those following vegan diets were less than half as likely to have developed diabetes than their meat eater counterparts [7]

- A 2010 literature review conducted by the Dietary Guidelines Advisory Committee showed that plant-based diets were associated with reduced risk of cardiovascular disease and mortality compared with non-plant-based diets [8]

- Studies have demonstrated that the removal or significant reduction of animal protein in the diet can slow and even halt the growth of cancerous cells [9]

While many people are initially impressed by this data, they are still left with questions. Here, we address some of the most common doubts people have before trying plant-based diets.

What About Protein?

Protein is one of three macronutrients found in food, along with carbohydrates and fat. It is made up of amino acids, which are found in all natural foods consumed by humans.

Many people falsely believe that animal products are necessary to obtain adequate amounts of protein. The truth is that a number of plant-based foods are high in protein, some even more so than meat. To prove that point, let's compare three popular animal-based products with three plant-based products by caloric content:

Food	Calories	Protein*
Bacon	100	6g
Steak	100	7g
Salmon	100	14g

Food	Calories	Protein*
Oatmeal	100	4g
Lentils	100	8g
Spinach	100	12g

*Approximate value

Seeds of Knowledge

Excessive amounts of Casein protein—found in dairy-based products such as milk, yogurt, ice cream, and more—have been shown in studies to accelerate cancer cell growth.[10] **Plants contain no casein protein and are packed with a tapestry of other nutrients that work in harmony with amino acids to give your body strength and vitality.**

Why hasn't my doctor told me any of this?

Only one in four doctors has received any type of nutrition training, and most of that training consists of one course in college. Translation? In our current system, there is a large disconnect between medicine and nutrition.

Where doctors truly ARE experts, however, is in prescription medicine, with medical schools offering ample courses for students to learn about drugs' impact on the body. While prescription medication is undoubtedly valuable, increased reliance on prescription medication means people will need doctors more than ever with each passing year.

What about calcium for strong bones?

We know that calcium helps make our bones strong. And for years, we've been told that in order to get calcium, we need to drink milk. But does the science actually support that claim?

The famous *Got Milk* ad campaign was not launched to educate people on the health benefits of drinking milk. In fact, the slogan was created by San Francisco ad agency Goodby, Silverstein & Partners to help revive declining milk sales in California in 1993. This type of corporate influence on mainstream nutrition knowledge is not at all uncommon.

The reality is that drinking milk is not proven to strengthen bones—in fact, it may do just the opposite. A cohort study conducted by Swedish scientists analyzed fracture rates among 61,433 women over a mean follow-up period of 20.1 years. Their findings? **Women with higher milk intakes had greater risks of fractures.**[11] If that wasn't disturbing enough, the women were also found to have higher rates of mortality. The same study also analyzed 45,339 men over a mean follow up period of 11.2 years. The men who consumed the most milk were also found to have higher rates of mortality and no reduced risk of fracture.

So if you're not consuming dairy, how can you get your calcium? Thankfully, nature has you covered.

A variety of plant-based foods contain ample amounts of calcium. Greens, seeds, beans, and nut butters are just some of the delicious options that allow you to build and maintain strong bones without the risks of dairy. What's more, these foods are incredibly energizing, giving you the boost to move more and, in turn, improve your skeletal structure.

I have a friend who failed on a plant-based diet. If the diet is so great, why did my friend only feel better after eating animal products again?

The only way to truly unlock the amazing benefits of a plant-based diet is to eat a variety of healthy foods—and enough of them. Many people fall into the traps of eating the same foods repeatedly, leaving them without ample nutrition, or simply not eating enough calories. For these people, familiar animal products simply fill in the gaps they were missing through their poor dietary choices. But unlike healthy plant-based foods, these animal products also come with a slew of downsides, making them a short-term fix at best.

Fortunately, the recipes you will find throughout this book incorporate a medley of delicious vegetables, fruits, whole grains, nuts, seeds, and legumes. We will introduce you to exciting new flavors while maintaining the comfort and familiarity of your favorite meals.

Can I Exercise on a Plant-Based Diet?

Chances are you don't follow the sport of Competitive Strongmen, but if you did, you'd know that perhaps the world's strongest man follows an entirely plant-based diet.

Patrik Baboumian, a 36-year-old athlete from Germany, began removing animal products from his diet in 2011. Since that time, he has earned the distinction of "Germany's Strongest Man" and set four Guinness World Records in the strength category. If you ever needed proof that someone can be strong by only eating plants, Patrik is your guy.

Across the globe, hundreds of thousands of everyday people succeed at the gym, on the roads, or in the weight room on plant-based diets. Many people attribute the anti-inflammatory effects of fruits and vegetables to faster workout recovery, greater stamina, and more explosive movements.

What About Honey?

At *Nature Has Flavor*, we strive to consume plant-based foods in their most natural form. In that sense, we believe honey—which stems from flower nectar—is nature's purest sweetener.

Other popular sweeteners in the plant-based dieting community come with a slew of issues. Agave nectar is a highly processed syrup, undergoing a heating process before finding its way into commercially available bottles. And brown rice syrup may contain high levels of inorganic arsenic, which can lead to a number of long-term health problems.

A Typical Day of Eating on a Plant-Based Diet

In our section on the standard Western diet, we explored what an average American would eat in a day following the United States food pyramid. Now, let's swap that diet for some of the healthy, plant-based recipes you will find in this booklet.

Woman

Morning

The woman starts her day with a serving of **Apple Spiced Oatmeal** (Day 3, Page 44) she prepared the night before. She is immediately energized from the early-morning infusion of nutrients, meaning she won't need to stop for a coffee on the way to work. With the extra time, she can help her kids get ready for school without feeling stressed and rushed.

At work, the woman is able to maintain high levels of concentration thanks to the slow-burning carbohydrates provided by her breakfast. Without the lumps of saturated fat from her usual cream cheese bagel in her system, her blood is flowing freely, leading to mental clarity and increased productivity. She forgoes her usual vending machine run and stays full until her lunch break.

Afternoon

At lunch, the woman goes into her work refrigerator to grab the **Tomato, Cucumber, and Red Onion Salad** (Day 2, Page 38) she had prepared the night before. The meal—packed with powerful antioxidants and nutrients—is refreshing after a productive morning at work. When her lunch break ends, she feels ready to continue her morning's progress. There is no major blood sugar crash that leaves her feeling tired and lethargic.

Evening

The woman goes home to begin preparing both tonight's dinner and tomorrow's breakfast and lunch. Tonight, the woman cooks with her children and husband, turning the **Butternut Squash Soup** (Day 1, Page 34) recipe into an opportunity for family bonding.

The ingredients in the soup, such as the Vitamin A-rich butternut squash and the selenium-rich garlic, have the entire family feeling amazing. Instead of watching TV after dinner, they decide to go for a brisk walk. The movement helps them wind down from their day, allowing them to fall asleep easier and feel refreshed the next morning.

Man

Morning

The man is the first to arrive at his early morning meeting, and he's feeling energetic and sharp. For breakfast, he had his new favorite dish—the Apple, Almond, and Date Charoset (Day 7, Page 68). With ample amounts of vitamins and minerals in his bloodstream, he looks and feels vibrant as he impresses his co-workers with his early-morning enthusiasm. On this morning, there's no need for the man to partake in the danishes offered on his conference table.

Afternoon

The man has been busy all morning, so his lunch break comes as a welcome reprieve. He goes to the office refrigerator where he has a container of White Bean and Pepper Salad (Day 8, Page 76) he had made two days earlier. Packed with clean protein, fiber, and antioxidants, the meal provides the man with the pick me up he needs to get through the afternoon. But unlike sugary, creamy coffee, the salad does not come with an energy crash.

The man finds himself hungry again around 3:00. It's been a busy day, and his body is requiring more fuel than usual. So he goes to the office freezer, where he has a bag of frozen pineapple chunks stored away. He eats a serving of the fruit and feels refreshed as he goes into the final few hours of his workday.

Evening

At 7:30 the man goes out to the bar with his co-workers. While the menu offers very few plant-based options, the man has a system in place: He orders a mixed greens salad, tops it with a baked potato, and flavors the combination with Tabasco sauce. The ingredients are simple, but the peppery Tabasco sauce provides enough of a punch to keep the man satisfied.

When the man returns home, his body feels satiated from the healthy foods he's consumed throughout the day. The thought of a late-night sugar rush does not even cross his mind.

Chapter 2

Preparing for the 21-Day Challenge

Depending on who you ask, switching to a plant-based diet will either be a seamless transition or a difficult uphill battle. The truth is, everyone is different, and how you handle this new journey will be based on any number of given variables.

Food is an important part of many cultures, and some people struggle with removing animal products from their staple dishes. Having received training at Le Cordon Bleu in London, I have always been incredibly passionate about French cuisine. When I switched to a plant-based diet, it was a daunting thought that I would no longer be enjoying meals with creamy sauces and cheeses.

Other people associate certain animal-based foods with happiness. Hot dogs and hamburgers are a staple part of cookouts. Ice cream often brings back fond childhood memories. And pizza has become our culture's go-to party food. For many, the thought of removing these foods from everyday life seems impossible.

Still, other people quickly thrive on a plant-based diet and never look back. You see, your body undergoes a number of changes when you start eating healthier, and often times that means your cravings will change as well. Instead of needing that burger, your body will yearn for flavorful, antioxidant-rich vegetables and legumes, which will energize you for the rest of your day.

But regardless of where you will fall on this spectrum, it is important that you give yourself every opportunity to succeed on this new journey. Chances are, you will struggle and sometimes slip up along the way. **But don't let your mistakes define how you move forward.**

At *Nature Has Flavor*, our sole goal is to help you succeed. If you have doubts or uncertainties, we guarantee many people have felt the exact same way. But we're confident that through dedication, smart dietary choices, and delicious plant-based meals, you will achieve your goals and live a happier, healthier lifestyle.

Cleaning Out Your Kitchen

Discipline is an admirable trait, but it requires a lot of energy to sustain. The best way to stay on track throughout your 21-Day Challenge is to make "discipline" as effortless as possible. **That's why your first step in preparing for the challenge is to rid your kitchen of all the foods that may tempt you to stray from your new diet.**

Many nutrition experts laud the detoxifying effects of a plant-based diet. By eating nature's healthiest foods, your body can more readily remove impurities, leaving you feeling refreshed and revitalized. Apply this philosophy when cleaning out your kitchen: The less junk food you have around you, the easier it will be to stay on course with your new diet.

Start with your freezer. Remove any frozen meat, fish, and dairy items. Call around to local food pantries, as many will accept frozen food donations.

Move to your refrigerator. Coffee creamers, cheeses, and toppings such as mayonnaise and sour cream all contain dairy. Other unlikely culprits are certain salad dressings like Ranch, French, and Thousand Island. Remove any cold cuts, eggs, butter, and ghee.

Continue with your cupboards. We will explore reading nutrition labels in detail in the next section of this chapter, but identifying if packaged items have dairy or egg content is actually quite simple. Because dairy and eggs are common food allergies, companies are required to explicitly state if their products contain either item at the bottom of all nutrition labels. If you see animal products listed on a product's label, package it for donation to a local food pantry.

You may still have some junk food lying around that happens to be free of animal products. But remember, the 21-Day Challenge isn't simply about removing animal products from your diet—it's also about replacing them with nature's most nutritious foods. Just as your body rids itself of toxins, you should rid your kitchen of soda, cookies, potato and tortilla chips, sugary cereals, and other snack-like items.

How to Shop—Navigating Supermarkets, Reading Nutrition Labels, and Restocking Your Kitchen

Many of the foods and spices you will use to restock your kitchen will be included as part of your *Nature Has Flavor, The Box* package, which can be purchased at naturehasflavor.com/plant-based-food-delivery. Included in The Box you will find the following:

- All extra virgin oils and vinegars
- Spices like black pepper, salt, cumin, chili pepper, and more
- A full shopping list of perishable food for 21 days
- An exclusive link to plant-based cooking instructional videos
- A welcome sheet with even more Nature Has Flavor exclusive content

Supermarkets across the United States share a similar setup, regardless of their franchisor. When shopping for healthy, plant-based foods, a good rule of thumb is to divide supermarkets into three sections:

- Sections where nearly all items are healthy (produce aisles, fruit and vegetable sections of the frozen food section)

- Sections that contain both healthy items and unhealthy items (pasta aisle, canned foods section, spices and sauces aisle, cereal aisle)

- Sections that contain almost entirely unhealthy items (deli, seafood section, aisle, bakery, dairy section, frozen TV dinners and dessert)

Reading Nutrition Labels

Every packaged food you will find at a supermarket includes a nutrition label and an ingredients list. Understanding these labels is relatively straightforward, but there are a few red flags you need to watch out for.

In the United States, labels are structured to include the following information:

- Fat content
- Saturated fat content
- Cholesterol content
- Sodium content
- Potassium content
- Protein content
- Vitamin A, C, and D content, calcium content, and iron content
- Remaining vitamin and mineral content
- Ingredients list
- General information on macronutrients and daily values
- Allergy information

Next to the amount of each nutrient is the percentage of that nutrient's Daily Value within a 2,000 calorie diet. This percentage is determined by the U.S. Food and Drug Administration (FDA).

When examining labels, you can use several tools to ensure what you're getting is plant-based and relatively healthy. We encourage everyone taking the 21-Day Challenge to put packaged foods through a three-question test:

1) Does the food contain cholesterol?

Dietary cholesterol is only found in significant amounts in animal products. Any food you purchase that contains cholesterol will not be entirely plant-based and therefore should be avoided.

2) Does the food contain milk or egg ingredients?

As you did during your kitchen cleanout, look for milk or egg ingredient warnings in the "ALLERGY INFORMATION" section towards the bottom of labels.

3) Are there more than three ingredients you can't pronounce?

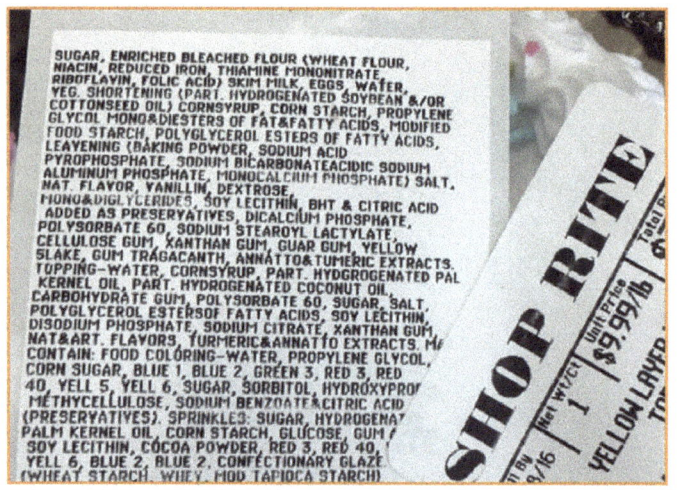

Ingredients of a simple birthday cake that would fail the "pronunciation test"

At *Nature Has Flavor*, we seek out ingredients that are as close to their natural form as possible. Unfortunately, this process has been made difficult by food companies, who add man-made preservatives and other processed ingredients to nearly every item they sell.

While it's impossible to avoid man-made ingredients entirely, we use a simple rule to limit our exposure to products made in a laboratory: If there are more than three ingredients we can't pronounce, we don't purchase the food. **Here are some of the most common additives to look out for:**

- Aspartame
- Butylated hydroxyanisole (BHA)
- Butylated hydroxytoluene (BHT)
- Guar Gum
- High Fructose Corn Syrup
- Monosodium Glutamate (MSG)
- Partially Hydrogenated Vegetable Oil (Trans Fat)
- Soy Lecithin
- Sucralose
- Tert-Butylhydroquinone (TBHQ)

Ingredients to avoid:

- Milk and milk proteins such as casein and whey (often referred to on labels as "dairy")
- Egg ingredients
- Seafood ingredients
- Meat ingredients
- Excessive artificial ingredients

Dealing with Skeptical Friends and Family

One of the most difficult parts of transitioning to a plant-based diet is dealing with family members and friends who don't understand or even respect your new way of eating. The best way to handle this challenge is with a steady blend of confidence and humility.

Chances are, someone in your life will ask you one of the questions we covered in the previous chapter of this book. When answering these questions, know that when you get past the many nutrition misconceptions our society has been led to believe, **the science is on your side**. In other words, you have every right to be confident when talking about the health benefits of your new diet.

Still, many people run into more subtle everyday challenges in dealing with loved ones on the plant-based lifestyle. Here, we outline some of the most common roadblocks you may face with friends and family and how to handle each situation.

The Issue: Loved ones taking offense to your not eating their cooking, which contains animal products.

The Solution: Let your loved ones know ahead of time about your new diet so it doesn't come as a surprise at the dinner table. It's more uncomfortable having to turn down food that has already been made than it is to let someone know ahead of time about your new dietary choices.

Tell your loved ones that you are undertaking this new diet to become a healthier, more energetic person, and that in turn, you will be a better husband, wife, daughter, son, etc. As much as you are making these changes for yourself, you are also making them for the people closest to you.

Additionally, your new diet will give you and your loved ones a unique opportunity to try new things together. If cooking is a big part of your family, bring this booklet into your kitchen and prepare a new recipe with those closest to you. Nature has afforded us with limitless flavor combinations, and many people only experience a fraction of them in their lifetime. Expanding your culinary horizons can be an exciting chance for you and your loved ones to become more cultured, adventurous, and knowledgeable about food.

The Issue: Going out to eat with friends and family at restaurants that primarily serve animal products.

The Solution: There are a number of ways to handle eating out on a plant-based diet, and putting together a solid plant-based meal is possible at just about any restaurant.

In today's era, more people are cutting out animal products from their diets than ever before, and restaurants are taking notice. Many restaurants cater specifically to plant-based dieters, offering a number of vegan-friendly options. Other restaurants will substitute dairy and meat-based products with plant-based foods upon request. There are a number of Internet blogs dedicated to helping readers find plant-based restaurants. A quick Google search will allow you to locate these restaurants in your area.

But even with many restaurants waking up to the plant-based movement, others still offer menus that place a heavy emphasis on animal-based products. Barbeque joints, steakhouses, and seafood restaurants are among the most guilty. When eating at these restaurants, it's still possible to stick to your plant-based approach—you just have to get creative.

One of the best ways to ensure you're avoiding animal products is by ordering simple foods. Salads, sides of potatoes, vegetables, and even grains can be combined to create a delicious plant-based meal. Oil and vinegar is a classic plant-based alternative to creamy salad dressings. Other ways to flavor your food include mustard, Tabasco sauce, moderate amounts of salt, pepper, and hot pepper flakes.

The Issue: Loved ones thinking your diet is "extreme."

The Solution: Many people consider plant-based diets to be "radical" or "unbalanced." But everything comes down to perspective. While some people may believe removing animal products from your diet is extreme, you can counter by saying that relying on prescription drugs and surgeries to maintain health is even *more* extreme. Ultimately, you are undertaking a healthy new lifestyle that has been proven to provide ample nutrition and flavor. Nothing is abnormal about that.

The Importance of Snacking

Between eating competitions, super-sized meals, and access to unprecedented amounts of food, our culture undoubtedly encourages overeating. Perhaps nothing summarizes this phenomenon more than the tongue-in-cheek Hawaiian saying, *"Here, we don't eat until we're full. We eat until we're tired."*

The meals included in the 21-Day Challenge will provide you with ample food and nutrition, but chances are, you won't experience that same feeling of "being stuffed" you'd get from downing a greasy burger and fries. While this lack of overindulgence is a fantastic part of plant-based dieting (post-meal fatigue often turns into sustained energy), many people have trouble getting used to a less-than-stuffed feeling.

The solution to these struggles is simple: Keep the right plant-based snacks handy at all times. Here are some simple rules to follow for healthy snacking:

1) Prepare ahead of time

Acknowledge the fact that you may get hungry at random points throughout the day and prepare accordingly. Stock your workplace refrigerator with lower sugar fruits like pineapple, raspberries, apples, and papaya. Keep several low-sugar granola bars in the glove compartment of your car. Wherever you know you'll be, make sure you have something healthy readily available—otherwise, you'll be forced to rely on vending machines and gas stations for snacks.

2) Don't become a sugar addict

While fruit can be an incredibly positive addition to your diet, the food group is notorious for its high sugar content. As a result, chugging a bottle of orange juice from concentrate is **not** the best way to handle your food cravings.

As far as snacking goes, we encourage you to choose fruits that are lower in sugar content. Below, we rank 10 of the most common fruits by sugar content:

One cup:

1) Raspberries 5g
2) Strawberries 7g
3) Apples 13g
4) Blueberries 15g
5) Pears 15g
6) Peaches 15g
7) Pineapple 16g
8) Oranges 17g
9) Mangoes 24g
10) Bananas 28g

By now, you know that plant-based diets can provide you with enough nutrition, variety, and flavor to live a healthy, happy life. Go into this new adventure with confidence and enthusiasm, and success will come your way!

Seeds of Knowledge

Buying frozen fruit and vegetables is a great way to ensure you always have a something healthy on hand. While fresh fruit and vegetables have a short shelf life, the flash-frozen variety you can buy at most supermarkets can last between 8-12 months at 0°F.[12]

And One Final Tip...Mise En Place

As you begin to embark on your new plant-based journey, we want to ensure you are able to prepare your meals as efficiently as possible. Whether you want to make cooking a family activity, or you are trying to prepare delicious, healthy food on a tight schedule, the most important rule of preparing food is organization. Chefs refer to this organization process as **Mise En Place**.

Before preparing a recipe in this book, we encourage you to take the following organizational steps. Doing so will save you time and make the cooking process all the more enjoyable.

1) Read the recipe in its entirety so you have a feel for the dish
2) Chop the vegetables you will need to prepare each dish
3) Ensure you have all of your ingredients and spices in place
4) Have this booklet handy for reference

Chapter 3

The Wonder of Nature's Flavors: A Nutritional Analysis of Common Plant-Based Foods

Fruits and vegetables are vibrant and full of color. But as beautiful as they may be to us, they are perhaps even more beautiful when examined under a microscope.

You see, inside of nearly every fruit, vegetable, nut, seed, and legume is a world of lively nutrients that can nourish the body on every level. We've always been told that plants are good for us—here are just some of the countless reasons why.

VEGETABLES

Vegetable	Family	Nutrition Highlights
Artichoke	Composite	Artichokes are rich in the mineral magnesium, which helps muscle and nerve function and serves as a key building block for healthy bones.[13] What's more, artichokes contain high levels of folate, helping the body metabolize amino acids.[14]
Arugula	Cruciferous	Arugula is an incredible, nutrient-dense food. An entire cup of arugula contains just 4 calories, yet it packs over 1/4 of your daily value of Vitamin K and 10% of your daily value of Vitamin A.
Asparagus	Asparagus	Low in calories and packed with vitamins and minerals, asparagus is a nutritional powerhouse. Just one cup of asparagus with your dinner will provide you with nearly 3/4 of your daily Vitamin C, over 60% of your daily folate, and a whopping 180% of your daily Vitamin K.
Beets	Goosefoot	Beets are so beneficial to the body that professional athletes are now using them in large amounts before competitions to gain an edge over their opponents. In addition to containing high amounts of folate and Vitamin C, beets are a strong source of dietary nitrates, which may help the body increase blood flow.
Bell Peppers	Nightshade	Bell peppers are among the richest sources of Vitamin C on earth, making them a powerful tool in staving off colds and oxidative stress. What's more, bell peppers provide an incredibly powerful flavor without a caloric surplus. In fact, an entire cup of chopped green bell peppers contains just 30 calories.

Vegetable	Family	Nutrition Highlights
Bok Choy	Cruciferous	Bok Choy, also referred to as Chinese cabbage, is just one of many vegetables that contains bone-building calcium. And there's an added benefit to getting your calcium from vegetables. According to Dr. Michael Greger, author of the best selling book *How Not to Die*, "calcium in dark green leafy vegetables like bok choy is absorbed about twice as well as the calcium in milk.".[15]
Brussel Sprouts	Cruciferous	When it comes to nutrition, brussel sprouts are among the most well-rounded vegetables in the world. Just some of the vitamins and minerals found in this cabbage vegetable: Vitamin B1, Vitamin B6, Vitamin C, Vitamin K, iron, manganese, and phosphorous.
Broccoli	Cruciferous	Broccoli's reputation as a healthy food is well earned. High in Vitamin C and Vitamin K, broccoli may help with iron absorption and blood clotting.[16][17] But what makes broccoli truly special is its detoxifying effects. Broccoli helps to produce more sulforaphane—a detoxifying enzyme produced by the liver—than any other plant on earth.[18]
Butternut Squash	Gourd	Just one cup of butternut squash provides roughly 450% of your daily value of Vitamin A, which can help you maintain a healthy immune system and strong eye sight.[19] Butternut Squash also contains a favorable Omega 3-to-Omega 6 ratio, which can help fight inflammation in the body.[20]
Cabbage	Cruciferous	A cup of cabbage contains just 22 calories, making the vegetable a nutritious addition to salads, soups, and more. Cabbage also contains glucosinolates, which, through a process in the body called hydrolysis, may help fight cancerous cells.[21]
Carrots	Umbelliferous	Carrots have long been considered a food for healthy eyes because of their high Vitamin A content. But what most people do not know is that carrots are also a strong source of potassium, Vitamin K, and dietary fiber, making them a well-rounded snack for when you're on the go.

Vegetable	Family	Nutrition Highlights
Cauliflower	Cruciferous	Cauliflower provides many of the same benefits as other cruciferous vegetables such as broccoli and cabbage while maintaining its own impressive nutritional profile. Just 25 calories worth of cauliflower will provide you with over 3/4 of your daily Vitamin C and over 10% of your daily dietary fiber, Vitamin K, Vitamin B6, and folate.
Celery	Umbelliferous	A study published in a 2012 edition of the *Proceedings of the Nutrition Society* concluded that it takes roughly 14 calories to digest 16 calories of celery.[22] This phenomenon makes celery an incredible snack for those looking to lose weight.
Cucumber	Gourd	Cucumbers are not only nutritious, containing solid amounts of Vitamin K and Vitamin C, but they are also incredibly hydrating. One cucumber weighing 301g contains roughly 287g of water, making the vegetable the perfect snack for a hot summer day.
Eggplant	Nightshade	While eggplants do not contain high levels of vitamins and minerals, they are a high-fiber, low-calorie vegetable, making them a tasty addition to plant-based meals. Eggplants also contain chlorogenic acid (CGA), which may help in fighting inflammation and oxidative stress.[23]
Kale	Cruciferous	One of the reasons kale has taken the health world by storm is because of its nutritional density. In addition to being a strong source of plant protein, kale is extremely high in Vitamin A, Vitamin C, and Vitamin K. It's also packed with potassium, Omega 3 fatty acids, copper, and manganese.
Lettuce	Composite	Comprised of roughly 95% water, lettuce is a hydrating, refreshing vegetable that also boasts an impressive nutritional profile. Just two cups of lettuce will provide you with roughly 165% of your daily Vitamin A and roughly 40% of your Vitamin C, all at just 16 calories.

Vegetable	Family	Nutrition Highlights
Onions	Allium	Onions contain high concentrations of Vitamin B6, an incredibly important vitamin that aids in protein metabolism. Onions are also a solid source of fiber, manganese, and Vitamin C.
Spinach	Goosefoot	Spinach is a mineral-rich green vegetable. Just two cups of spinach will provide you with over 10% of your daily iron, magnesium, potassium, and manganese. And like other greens, spinach packs large amounts of Vitamin A, Vitamin C, and Vitamin K.
Sweet Potatoes	Morning Glory	When it comes to getting your daily nutrition, sweet potatoes may be the most versatile vegetable in the world. Here's just a sampling of the vitamins and minerals you'll find in sweet potatoes: Vitamin A, Vitamin C, Vitamin B1, Vitamin B2, Vitamin B3, Vitamin B5, Vitamin B6, magnesium, phosphorous, potassium, copper, and manganese.
Yellow Squash and Zucchini	Gourd	Yellow squash and zucchini, which are sometimes referred to as summer squash, are potassium powerhouses. Just half of a squash contains roughly 15% of your daily potassium while containing only 25-30 calories. Squash is also a good source of Vitamin B2, Vitamin B6, and folate.

NATURE HAS FLAVOR

Fruit	Family	Nutrition Highlights
Apple	Rose	Whole apples are an antioxidant powerhouse, containing some 5,609 antioxidant units per fruit. What's more, apples contain high amounts of fiber, making them a satiating snack when you're on the go.
Applesauce (Unsweetened)	Rose	Applesauce can serve as a healthy snack when you are craving something naturally sweet. It contains moderate amounts of Vitamin C and fiber and is very low in fat. Be sure to purchase the unsweetened versions of applesauce, as many brands unnecessarily add syrups and sugars to what is an already flavorful food.
Avocado	Laurel	There's a reason why avocados are a staple food in the *Nature Has Flavor 21-Day Challenge*: They're among the healthiest and most versatile foods on earth. Loaded with potassium, pantothenic acid (an essential nutrient that aids in nutrient metabolism[24]), and ample amounts of other healthy minerals, avocados can be a nourishing base for spreads, salads, and even desserts.
Bananas	Banana	While bananas are best known for their potassium content, perhaps what makes this fruit so special that it shares roughly 60% of its DNA with humans.[25] When you eat bananas, you're loading your body with electrolytes, water, and loads of vitamins and minerals.
Blackberries	Rose	Blackberries contain more antioxidants than any other popular berry in the United States (only several types of exotic berries contain more antioxidants). They're also packed with fiber, Vitamin K, and several key minerals including manganese and copper.
Blueberries	Heath	Though they are low in calories and full of powerful antioxidants, perhaps what's most exciting about blueberries is their potential medicinal properties. Blueberries contain anthocyanin pigments, which, according to a 2004 study in the *Journal of Biomedicine and Biotechnology*, "have demonstrated ability to protect against a myriad of human diseases."[26]

Fruit	Family	Nutrition Highlights
Cantaloupe	Gourd (Melon)	Like most melons, cantaloupe contains high amounts of water, making it an ideal food for hydration. Cantaloupe is highly nutritious as well. Just one cup will provide you with 120% of your daily Vitamin A, 108% of your daily Vitamin C, and 14% of your daily potassium.
Cherry	Rose	Cherries are listed as one of the American Institute for Cancer Research's "Foods that Fight Cancer."[27] Full of powerful antioxidants such as anthocyanins, cherries are a delicious way to fight stress.[28] But be careful when shopping for cherries, as some brands combine the fruit in processed sugars and syrups.
Coconut	Arecaceae	Coconuts contain a rare type of fat called medium chain triglycerides (MCTs), which are quickly metabolized by the liver and used for energy. Coconut milk is also similar in texture and consistency to cow's milk, providing a plant-based alternative to a number of dairy dishes.[29]
Dates	Palm	A 2003 study in the *International Journal of Food Sciences and Nutrition* said dates are "almost an ideal food, providing a wide range of essential nutrients and potential health benefits."[30] Packed with vitamins and minerals, dates can nourish your body while satisfying your sweet tooth.
Grapes	Grape	Grapes provide well-rounded nutrition, containing notable amounts of Vitamin C and the mineral copper, which can help the body utilize iron and maintain healthy cholesterol levels.[31]
Grapefruit	Citrus	Grapefruit, like most citrus fruits, is high in Vitamin C content, containing roughly 120% of your daily value per just 97 calories. Grapefruit also contains notable amounts of fiber and potassium, as well as small, but not insignificant amounts of several B vitamins.

Fruit	Family	Nutrition Highlights
Kiwi	Kiwi	Kiwis are yet another nutritionally well-rounded fruit, providing a variety of key nutrients without excess calories. One cup of kiwis will provide you with 273% of your daily Vitamin C, 89% of your daily Vitamin K, and 16% of your daily potassium, all while containing just 108 calories.
Lemon	Citrus	Lemons are truly an incredible fruit. In a 2002 study published in the *Journal of Agricultural and Food Chemistry*, lemons were found to actually inhibit the proliferation of human liver cancer cells in vitro.[32] With loads of flavor per drop of lemon juice, adding lemons to your plant-based diet is a no brainer.
Lime	Citrus	A single lime can provide you with roughly 30% of your daily Vitamin C while only containing 20 calories. Like lemons, limes pack ample amounts of flavor in every bite, making them a healthy addition to your salads, beverages, desserts, and more.
Mangoes	Cashew	Perhaps the greatest nutritional quality of mangoes is the fruit's high Vitamin B6 content. Eating one mango will provide you with roughly 15% of your daily Vitamin B6, which plays a role in immune function, cognitive development, and hemoglobin formation.[33] Mangoes are also packed with Vitamin C, Vitamin A, and Vitamin E.
Oranges	Citrus	While oranges are best known for their high Vitamin C content, the flavorful fruit is also a solid source of Vitamin B1, folate, and potassium. Whole oranges also contain fiber, making the whole fruit a more nutritious option than concentrated orange juice.
Papaya	Papaya	In addition to being highly nutritious, papayas contain rare enzymes called papains, which may aid in digestion and allow you to better absorb nutrients from the rest of your diet.[34] The most notable nutrients in papaya include Vitamin C, Vitamin A, and folate.

Fruit	Family	Nutrition Highlights
Peach	Rose	Like many fruits on this list, peaches are high in Vitamin C, Vitamin A, and potassium, making them a nutritious snack or addition to salads, cereals, and more. Peaches may also have protective qualities for our visual health. In a 2012 study published in the *American Journal of Ophthalmology*, women who consumed at least one serving of peaches per week were found to have a 47% decreased risk of glaucoma than women who consumed less than one serving of peaches per month.
Pear	Rose	Pears are more fibrous than most fruits, containing 22% of your daily fiber per medium piece of fruit. What's more, pears contain phenolics and flavonoid contents that were found to have anti-inflammatory effects in a 2012 study published in the *Journal of Agricultural and Food Chemistry*.[35]
Plum	Rose	In 2008, Dr. Michael Greger, author of the best-selling *How Not to Die*, ranked plums as the ninth best food in the world for antioxidant content.[36] With some 5,000 antioxidant units per one black plum, it's easy to see why Dr. Greger made this choice. Plums are also low in calories, with only 30 calories per fruit.
Pineapple	Pineapple	Pineapple is packed with Vitamin C, B vitamins, and potassium, making it an incredibly energizing fruit. Pineapple is also the only food on earth to naturally contain bromelain, a protein which may fight inflammation.[37]
Raspberry	Rose	Raspberries are incredibly fibrous, containing roughly 32% of your daily fiber per cup. What's more, raspberries are very low in calories, making them an ideal snack when you're craving something sweet.
Strawberry	Rose	Strawberries are among the most important fruits on a plant-based diet, as they are one of the only plants in the world to contain significant amounts of iodine, a key nutrient in regulating thyroid function and more.[38] And like other fruits, strawberries are an excellent source of water, Vitamin C, and fiber.

Fruit	Family	Nutrition Highlights
Watermelon	Gourd (Melon)	Watermelon, unsurprisingly, is an incredibly hydrating fruit, consisting of roughly 93% water weight. Watermelon also contains small, but not insignificant amounts of minerals such as phosphorous, magnesium, and potassium, as well as high Vitamin C and Vitamin A levels.

NUTS, SEEDS, AND LEGUMES

Food	Family	Nutrition Highlights
Almonds	Nut	Almonds contain high levels of protein, manganese, and the potent antioxidant Vitamin E, making them among the most nutrient and mineral-dense nuts in the world. But what really makes almonds special are their high levels of calcium, making them a valuable tool for bone health.
Black Beans	Legume	Black beans are a mineral powerhouse, containing high levels of iron, magnesium, phosphorous, potassium, zinc, copper, and manganese, just to name a few. Black beans are also an excellent source of plant-based protein, packing 15 grams of the macronutrient per one-cup serving.
Brazil Nuts	Nut	Brazil nuts are so high in the mineral selenium that just one serving will provide you with 767% of your daily value. And incredibly, a 2013 study in the *Department of Chemistry, Natural and Exact Sciences Centers* observed that just one serving of Brazil Nuts was able to lower the "bad" cholesterol of test subjects for up to 30 days after consumption (servings ranged from 5g to 50g of the nut).[39]
Cashews	Nut	Nutritionally, cashews are a well-rounded nut, providing high levels of protein, iron, and a number of essential minerals. What's more, cashews are relatively low in saturated fat compared to other nuts, containing only 11% of your daily value per 1 oz serving.

NUTS, SEEDS, AND LEGUMES

Food	Family	Nutrition Highlights
Chia Seeds	Seed	Chia seeds are among the top plant-based sources of Omega 3 fatty acids, which have been found in a number of studies to help cognitive function, fight inflammation, and more.[40] Chia seeds also contain high levels of calcium, packing 18% of your daily value per 1 oz serving.
Fava Beans	Legume	Just one cup of boiled fava beans will provide you with 37% of your daily fiber and 44% of your daily folate, making them a go-to food for solid digestion and amino acid metabolism. And like other legumes, fava beans contain high levels of a number of other minerals including magnesium, phosphorous, potassium, zinc, copper, and manganese.
Flax Seeds	Seed	Just how healthy are flax seeds? Dr. Caldwell Esselstyn, one of the foremost authorities on plant-based nutrition in the world, encourages followers of a plant-based diet to eat a tablespoon of flax seed meal every day.[41] As flax seeds contain high levels of Omega 3 fatty acids, Vitamin B1, and more, it's easy to see why Dr. Esselstyn makes this recommendation.
Garbanzo Beans (Chickpeas)	Legume	Garbanzo beans, like other legumes, are nutritionally well-rounded, containing high levels of fiber, solid amounts of plant-based protein, and a number of vitamins and minerals. But perhaps what stands out most among chickpeas' nutritional profile is their high level of iron, an essential mineral which assists with everything from cellular functioning to oxygen transportation in the bloodstream.[42]
Green Beans	Legume	Green beans are a unique culinary legume, as we are able to eat them within their protective pod. For those who are not a fan of other legumes, green beans are a great way to obtain a number of minerals such as manganese and potassium, as well as high levels of fiber. Green beans are also comprised of roughly 90% water, making them a hydrating addition to your meals.

NUTS, SEEDS, AND LEGUMES

Food	Family	Nutrition Highlights
Hazelnuts	Nut	Hazelnuts are a favorite among many nutritionists because they contain less saturated fat than nearly any other nut on earth. Loaded with vitamins, minerals, protein, and fiber, hazelnuts are a great choice to obtain optimum nutrition while reducing overall saturated fat intake.
Kidney Beans	Legume	Kidney beans might be the ultimate food for rejuvenation. Just one cup of cooked kidney beans contains 15g of protein, 52% of your daily dietary fiber, and over 20% of a number of your daily vitamins and minerals. What's even more impressive, just one cup of dark red kidney beans contains 8,045 antioxidant units per 3.5 oz, making the legumes among the most powerful foods in the world at fighting oxidation.
Lentils	Legume	There's a reason lentils have stood the test of time in the kitchen—they're incredibly good for you. Packed with ample amounts of fiber, folate, Vitamin B1, iron, and more, lentils have been fueling healthy people for thousands of years.
Macadamia Nuts	Nut	Macadamia nuts are very high in fat, meaning you shouldn't eat them in excess. However, the nuts are very nutrient-rich, providing diverse minerals and high levels of Vitamin B1, which is essential for the growth and formation of new cells.[43]
Peanuts	Legume	Both peanuts and peanut butter are good sources of plant-based protein and a number of essential minerals. Peanuts are also very high in Vitamin B3, which can help with digestion and nerve function.[44]
Pecans	Nut	While pecans do not contain large amounts of any one vitamin or mineral, they are a rich source of antioxidants, containing 17,524 antioxidant units per 3.5 oz. Pecans are also relatively fibrous, containing 11% of your daily dietary fiber per 1 oz serving.

NUTS, SEEDS, AND LEGUMES

Food	Family	Nutrition Highlights
Pinto Beans	Legume	Pinto beans contain high levels of protein, packing over 15 g per one cup serving. They're also full of nutrients, containing high levels of B vitamins and various minerals.
Pistachios	Nut	Pistachios are great fighters of oxidation in the body, containing 7,295 antioxidant units per 3.5 oz. Pistachios also contain 6g of protein per 1 oz serving and serve as a solid source of B vitamins, phosphorous, copper, and manganese.
Pumpkin Seeds	Seed	Pumpkin seeds are prized for their high zinc content. A relatively elusive mineral in food, zinc serves a number of important functions in the body including boosting immune function and wound healing.[45] Pumpkin seeds also provide high levels of protein, magnesium, and copper.
Sesame Seeds	Seed	Sesame seeds are yet another great source of plant-based calcium, providing 27% of your daily value per 1 oz serving. Sesame seeds also pack high levels of several B vitamins and provide over 20% of your daily value for seven key minerals.
Soybeans	Legume	Prized by plant-based chefs around the world for their culinary versatility, soybeans are also a nutritional juggernaut. Perhaps the best source of plant-based protein on this list, soybeans are also a significant source of iron, dietary fiber, and numerous vitamins and minerals.
Sunflower Seeds/Butter	Seed/Spread	Sunflower seeds and sunflower butter (ground sunflower seeds made into a spread) contain very high levels of Vitamin E, which is an important nutrient for immune function.[46] Just one serving of sunflower seeds also contains over 30% of your daily value for phosphorous, magnesium, and selenium, and over 40% of your daily value for copper and manganese.
Walnuts	Nut	In a 2010 study published in the *Journal of the American College of Nutrition*, walnuts were said to have "cardioprotective effects", making them a good choice for those concerned about their heart health.[47] Perhaps the reason walnuts are so healthy is their high levels of Omega 3 and Omega 6 fatty acids, as well their rich mineral content.

NATURE HAS FLAVOR

References

1. http://www.diabetes.org/diabetes-basics/statistics/
2. http://www.cdc.gov/nchs/fastats/body-measurements.htm
3. http://www.cdc.gov/heartdisease/facts.htm
4. http://www.cdc.gov/dhdsp/data_statistics/fact_sheets/fs_cholesterol.htm
5. http://www.health.harvard.edu/heart-health/halt-heart-disease-with-a-plant-based-oil-free-diet-
6. http://www.ncbi.nlm.nih.gov/pubmed/1973470/
7. http://www.ncbi.nlm.nih.gov/pmc/articles/PMC2671114
8. http://www.ncbi.nlm.nih.gov/pmc/articles/PMC3662288/#b26-permj17_2p0061
9. http://ajcn.nutrition.org/content/85/6/1667.long
10. http://www.ncbi.nlm.nih.gov/pmc/articles/PMC4166373/
11. http://www.ncbi.nlm.nih.gov/pubmed/25352269
12. http://nchfp.uga.edu/how/freeze/freezer_shelf_life.html
13. https://ods.od.nih.gov/factsheets/Magnesium-HealthProfessional/
14. https://ods.od.nih.gov/factsheets/Folate-HealthProfessional/
15. http://nutritionfacts.org/video/plant-vs-cow-calcium-2/
16. https://ods.od.nih.gov/factsheets/VitaminC-HealthProfessional/
17. https://ods.od.nih.gov/factsheets/VitaminK-HealthProfessional/
18. http://nutritionfacts.org/video/the-best-detox/
19. https://ods.od.nih.gov/factsheets/VitaminA-HealthProfessional/
20. http://www.ncbi.nlm.nih.gov/pubmed/12442909
21. http://lpi.oregonstate.edu/mic/food-beverages/cruciferous-vegetables
22. http://journals.cambridge.org/action/displayAbstract?fromPage=online&aid=8888281&fileId=S0029665112003084
23. https://www.researchgate.net/publication/269708853_Breeding_for_Chlorogenic_Acid_Content_in_Eggplant_Interest_and_Prospects
24. http://umm.edu/health/medical/altmed/supplement/vitamin-b5-pantothenic-acid
25. https://www.genome.gov/dnaday/q.cfm?aid=785&year=2010
26. http://www.ncbi.nlm.nih.gov/pmc/articles/PMC1082894/
27. http://www.aicr.org/foods-that-fight-cancer/
28. http://www.aicr.org/foods-that-fight-cancer/foodsthatfightcancer/cherries.html
29. http://jn.nutrition.org/content/132/3/329.full
30. http://www.ncbi.nlm.nih.gov/pubmed/12850886
31. https://ods.od.nih.gov/News/Copper.aspx
32. http://www.ncbi.nlm.nih.gov/pubmed/12452674
33. https://ods.od.nih.gov/factsheets/VitaminB6-HealthProfessional/
34. https://hort.purdue.edu/newcrop/morton/papaya_ars.html
35. http://www.ncbi.nlm.nih.gov/pubmed/22880800
36. http://nutritionfacts.org/video/antioxidant-content-of-300-foods-2/
37. https://www.ncbi.nlm.nih.gov/pmc/articles/PMC538506/
38. https://www.mskcc.org/cancer-care/patient-education/low-iodine-diet
39. https://www.researchgate.net/publication/248385213_A_Single_Consumption_of_High_Amounts_of_the_Brazil_Nuts_Improves_Lipid_Profile_of_Healthy_Volunteers

References

40. http://umm.edu/health/medical/altmed/supplement/omega3-fatty-acids
41. http://www.choose-healthy-eating-for-life.com/heart-healthy-diet.html#.VyZZD3qzlCx
42. https://ods.od.nih.gov/factsheets/Iron-HealthProfessional/
43. https://ods.od.nih.gov/factsheets/Thiamin-HealthProfessional/
44. https://www.nlm.nih.gov/medlineplus/ency/article/002409.htm
45. https://ods.od.nih.gov/factsheets/Zinc-HealthProfessional/
46. https://ods.od.nih.gov/factsheets/VitaminE-HealthProfessional/
47. http://www.ncbi.nlm.nih.gov/pubmed/21677123

*All data regarding nutritional values of each food was obtained from NutritionData.Self.Com, which sources its data from the United States Department of Agriculture (USDA). All data regarding antioxidant content of food obtained from the USDA Database for the Oxygen Absorbance Radical Capacity of Selected Foods, Release 2

Nature Has Flavor's Recipes for the 21-Day Challenge

Breakfast | **DAY 1**

Avocado and Tomato Toast

Makes 2 Servings

Ingredients

1 ripe avocado, sliced open, pit removed

2 ripe tomatoes, sliced into 1/4 inch thick slices

1/2 cup baby spinach, washed

4 slices whole wheat/or whole grain bread, toasted (please do not use white bread)

NHF kosher salt, as needed

NHF course ground black pepper, as needed

4 teaspoons NHF balsamic vinegar

Method

1. Remove the avocado meat into a bowl using a spoon.
2. Mash the avocado with a fork and season with salt and pepper; taste and set aside.
3. Season the tomatoes with salt and pepper; set aside.
4. On each piece of toast, spread 1/4 of the seasoned avocado and drizzle 1 teaspoon of balsamic vinegar; spread the vinegar into the avocado.
5. Top the avocado with a few spinach leaves, allotting enough avocado for the remaining pieces of toast.
6. Top the spinach with the sliced tomatoes and serve.

Lunch | **DAY 1**

Butternut Squash Soup

Makes 4 Servings

Ingredients

For the soup:

16 oz butternut squash, peeled and diced large

8 oz sweet potato, peeled and diced large

1/2 Spanish onion, peeled and diced large

2 celery stalks, diced large

1 large carrot, peeled and diced large

NHF kosher salt, as needed

NHF butcher ground black pepper, as needed

NHF extra virgin olive oil, as needed

2 teaspoons NHF ground cinnamon

4 garlic cloves

1 cup white wine

Water, as needed

For the garnish:

2 teaspoons NHF truffle oil (optional)

NHF kosher salt, as needed

1 tablespoons chives, chopped

1/4 cup pumpkin seeds, toasted

Method

For the soup:

1. Place a soup pot over high heat. Once the pot is hot, add extra virgin olive oil.

2. Add the squash, sweet potatoes, onions, carrots, potatoes and celery. Stir well and cook over high heat for 4 minutes.

3. Add the garlic and season with some salt and pepper.

4. Add the cinnamon sticks and stir. Add the wine, bring to a boil, and reduce the liquids by half.

5. Add enough water to cover the vegetables, bring back to a boil, and cook over medium heat for 25 minutes or until fork tender.

6. Remove from heat and remove the cinnamon sticks. Using a drink or a stick blender, mix the chunky soup into a smooth, textured soup.

7. Please blend the soup carefully. You will need to let each batch run for about 2-3 minutes to reach the desired consistency. Remove from the blender into a clean pot.

8. Once you blend the soup, place the pot on low heat. Adjust seasoning with salt and pepper and the thickness by adding water if needed. Please note that the consistency should be such that when you dip a spoon in the soup, the soup will stick to the spoon.

9. Do not boil the soup—simply bring it to a hot temperature and serve immediately.

For the garnish:

1. Place the soup in a bowl and place some toasted pumpkin seeds in the center of the soup.

2. Drizzle some truffle oil around the pumpkin seeds, then sprinkle some chopped chives and serve.

Dinner | **DAY 1**

Roasted Vegetable Risotto

Makes 2 Servings

Ingredients

For the rice:

1/2 pint Arborio rice

1 quarts vegetable stock

1 cup white wine

NHF ground white pepper, as needed

NHF kosher salt, as needed

1/2 cup Spanish onion, chopped

2 ounces sunflower butter

2 ounces unsweetened apple sauce

1 tablespoon olive oil

1 tablespoon of chives, finely chopped

For the vegetables:

1/2 red onion, cut into 8 wedges

8 pieces Brussel sprouts cut in 1/2

1/2 red pepper, medium dice

1/2 zucchini, medium dice

1/2 yellow squash, medium dice

1 tablespoons NHF extra virgin olive oil

2 tablespoons NHF balsamic vinegar

NHF kosher salt, as needed

NHF course ground black pepper, as needed

Method

For the rice:

1. Place a deep saucepan over medium heat.
2. Add the olive oil and the onions and sauté until translucent.
3. Add the Arborio rice and stir well. Season with salt and pepper and mix well.
4. Add the white wine and cook over medium heat until reduced by 1/2. Start adding vegetable stock to the risotto, 2 cups at a time, making sure that you stir the risotto continuously and that all of the liquid has evaporated before adding more stock.
5. The amount of vegetable stock and time of cooking may change due to variables such as kitchen temperature, humidity, pan quality, and the strength of the stove. Please taste the risotto before making any decisions as to doneness.
6. Just before the risotto has absorbed all of its liquid, add sunflower butter and apple sauce, and continue to stir.
7. When done, remove from the heat. Stir in the chopped chives just before serving with the roasted vegetables.

For the vegetables:

1. Preheat oven to 400°F.
2. Place all of the vegetables on a sheet pan, season with salt, pepper, extra virgin olive oil, and balsamic vinegar.
3. Roast the vegetables for 15 to 20 minutes, or until tender.
4. Serve the roasted vegetables atop the risotto.

Breakfast | **DAY 2**

Tomato, Cucumber Red Onion Salad

Makes 2 Servings

Ingredients

30 ripe grape tomatoes, sliced in 1/2

1/2 red onion, peeled and sliced into **1/8** inch slices (thin slices)

1 English cucumber, peeled and sliced into 1/4 inch slices

1 ripe avocado, sliced open, pit removed, scooped and sliced into 1/4 inch slices

10 Kalamata olives, pitted, sliced in 1/2

1 lemon, juiced, pits removed

2 teaspoons NHF Italian seasoning

1 tablespoon NHF extra virgin olive oil

NHF kosher salt, as needed (1 teaspoon suggested)

NHF course ground black pepper, as needed (1 teaspoon suggested)

Optional - 2 slices of whole grain bread, toasted – try to do without the bread, but if you feel that your body needs it, feel free to use.

Method

1. Combine the tomatoes, cucumbers, red onions, and Kalamata olives in a large bowl.

2. Add the lemon juice, olive oil, and Italian seasoning, and toss together.

3. Season the salad with salt and pepper. Adjust seasoning if you desire stronger flavor.

4. Divide the salad into 2 salad bowls; pour the dressing over the salad equally between the plates.

5. Place the avocado slices (1/2 avocado per serving) atop the salad and serve.

Lunch | DAY 2

Carrot Pilaf with Roasted Asparagus and Tahini Sauce

Makes 2 Servings

Ingredients

For the rice:

2 large carrots, peeled and grated

1 medium Spanish onion, peeled and diced small

2 garlic cloves, peeled and sliced thin

1 cup basmati rice

2 cups of water

NHF kosher salt, as needed

NHF course ground black pepper, as needed

2 teaspoons NHF ground cumin

2 teaspoons NHF ground paprika

1 teaspoon NHF ground turmeric

1 tablespoon NHF extra virgin olive oil

For the asparagus:

1 lb asparagus, cut off the stem, washed and dried

2 teaspoons NHF kosher salt

2 tablespoons NHF extra virgin olive oil

For the tahini sauce:

1 cup tahini paste

2 tablespoons freshly squeezed lemon juice

1 whole clove of garlic

2 teaspoons NHF kosher salt

1 teaspoon NHF ground white pepper

About 1/2 - 1 cup of water

Method

For the rice:

1. In a medium-size sauce pan over medium-high heat, add the olive oil.
2. Add the onions and sweat on until light brown in color.
3. Add the carrots and keep cooking until soft and caramelized.
4. Add the garlic and cook for 1 minute.
5. Add the rice and stir well.
6. Add the cumin, paprika, turmeric, salt (2 teaspoons), and black pepper. Stir well.
7. Add the water and taste. It should taste as salty as ocean water (if it doesn't, add a little more salt).
8. Turn up to high heat and bring to a boil.
9. Once it boils, turn to low heat, cover well, and cook for 17 minutes.
10. Remove from heat and let the rice sit covered for 5 minutes.
11. Remove the cover and fluff the rice with a fork. Set aside in a warm place.

For the asparagus:

1. Preheat the oven to 475°F.
2. Place the asparagus on a sheet pan, season with salt and drizzle with olive oil.
3. Place the pan into the oven's middle rack.
4. Cook the asparagus for 10 minutes. Remove the pan carefully, as the asparagus might be smoky, and stir the asparagus around.
5. Be sure to flip the asparagus over. Return the pan to the oven and cook for 3-5 more minutes until golden brown.
6. Remove from the oven, check seasoning and place in a warm place.

For the tahini sauce:

1. Place the tahini paste, garlic, lemon juice, salt and pepper into a food processor bowl.
2. Start working the machine and drizzle the water. Start with a 1/2 cup of water and check the consistency.
3. The sauce should coat the back of a spoon, but not be too thick. If you want the sauce thinner, add some water and work the machine again.
4. Once you have reached the desired consistency, remove from the food processor into a container and set aside.

For the assembly:

1. Place the rice onto 2 serving plates; add the asparagus next to it.
2. Serve the tahini on the side as a dipping sauce, or atop the rice.

Dinner | DAY 2

Creamy Cauliflower Soup

Makes 4 Servings

Ingredients

For the soup:

16 oz cauliflower florets, cleaned

8 oz Yukon gold potatoes, peeled and diced large

1 Spanish onion, peeled and diced large

2 celery stalks, diced large

3 tablespoons dill, chopped

1 tablespoon NHF kosher salt

1 teaspoon NHF course ground black pepper

2 tablespoons NHF extra virgin olive oil

2 garlic cloves

1 cup white wine

Water, as needed

For the garnish:

2 teaspoons NHF lemon infused extra virgin olive oil (optional)

1 tablespoon dill, chopped

Method

For the soup:

1. Place a soup pot over high heat. Once the pot is hot, add extra virgin olive oil.
2. Add the cauliflower, potatoes, onions and celery. Stir well and cook over medium high heat for 5 minutes.
3. Add the garlic and season with some salt and pepper.
4. Add the dill and stir. Add the wine, bring to a boil and reduce the liquids by half.
5. Add enough water to cover the vegetables, bring back to a boil and cook for 25 minutes or until fork tender over medium heat.
6. Remove from heat. Using a drink or a stick blender, mix the chunky soup into a smooth textured soup.
7. Please blend the soup carefully. You will need to let each batch run for about 2-3 minutes to reach the desired consistency. Remove from the blender into a clean pot.
8. Once you blend all the soup, place the pot on low heat. Adjust seasoning with salt and pepper and adjust the thickness by adding water if needed. Please note that the consistency should be such that when you dip a spoon in the soup, the soup will stick to the spoon.
9. Do not boil the soup—simply bring it to a hot temperature and serve immediately.

For the garnish:

1. Place the soup in a bowl, drizzle some lemon infused extra virgin olive oil, then sprinkle some chopped dill and serve.

Breakfast | **DAY 3**

Apple Spiced Oatmeal

Makes 2 Servings

Ingredients

For the oatmeal:

1 cup quick oats

1 3/4 cups water

2 oz apple sauce, no sugar added (1 individual container)

1 teaspoon dark agave nectar

1 teaspoon NHF ground cinnamon

For the garnish:

4 walnut halves, crushed (optional)

1/2 red apple, small dice

2 strawberries, small dice

2 teaspoons dark agave nectar

Method

For the oatmeal:

1. Place the oatmeal and water in a small pot.
2. Add the agave nectar and cinnamon and stir well.
3. Turn on the stovetop to medium high heat and bring to a boil. When the contents begin boiling, reduce the heat to low and cook for 1 minute.
4. Remove from the heat and stir in the apple sauce; incorporate into the oatmeal.
5. Place in a warm place until ready to serve.

For the garnish:

1. Divide the oatmeal into 2 bowls. Place half of the red apple and the strawberries in the center in a small pile.
2. Sprinkle the crushed walnuts atop the oatmeal.
3. Drizzle the agave nectar around and atop the fruits and serve.

Lunch | DAY 3

Roasted Sweet Potato Sandwich

Makes 2 Servings

Ingredients

For the roasted sweet potato:

1 large sweet potato, peeled and sliced into 1/4 inch slices

1 tablespoon fresh ginger, crushed and chopped

1 tablespoon NHF extra virgin olive oil

2 teaspoons NHF kosher salt

1 teaspoon NHF course ground black pepper

2 teaspoons NHF Italian seasoning

2 tablespoons plant based mayonnaise

4 slices whole wheat/or whole grain bread, toasted (please do not use white bread)

For the assembly:

1 ripe tomato, sliced into about 1/4 inch slices

1/4 red onion, thinly sliced

1/2 cup arugula

1 tablespoon NHF balsamic vinegar

Method

For the roasted sweet potato:

1. Preheat oven to 400°F.
2. Brush a sheet pan with a little extra virgin olive oil.
3. Place the sweet potato slices on the pan and brush them with some olive oil.
4. Sprinkle the ginger, Italian seasoning and salt and pepper, and drizzle with some more olive oil.
5. Place inside the oven, in the middle rack, and cook uncovered for 15-20 minutes.
6. Please check about every 5 minutes to make sure that the potatoes do not burn; we are looking for a golden brown color. Make sure to turn the potatoes over after 7 minutes.
7. One the potatoes are al dente (85% cooked and not completely fork tender), remove from the oven.
8. Remove the potatoes from the pan onto a plate and set aside in a cool place.

For the assembly:

1. Toss the arugula with the balsamic vinegar and set aside.
2. Spread 2 tablespoons of vegan mayonnaise over 4 slices of bread.
3. Place a handful of arugula on one side of the bread.
4. Top with 2 slices of tomatoes, then the roasted sweet potatoes.
5. Add the sliced red onions and top with the 2nd slice of bread.
6. Slice the sandwich in 1/2 and serve.

Dinner | **DAY 3**

Tomato Soup

Makes 4 Servings

Ingredients

For the soup:

16 oz crushed tomatoes (canned)

1 Spanish onion, peeled and medium diced

3 large carrots, grated

1 cup basil, roughly chopped

1 tablespoon NHF kosher salt

1 teaspoon NHF course ground black pepper

1 tablespoon NHF sweet paprika

2 tablespoons NHF extra virgin olive oil

2 garlic cloves, chopped

1 cup carrot juice

1 cup white wine (Chablis or any other semi sweet wine)

Water, as needed

For the garnish:

2 teaspoons NHF extra virgin olive oil (optional)

10 basil leaves, chiffonade (long strips)

Method

For the soup:

1. Place a soup pot over high heat. Once the pot is hot, add extra virgin olive oil.
2. Add the onions and carrots. Stir well and cook over medium heat for 5-7 minutes.
3. Add the garlic and season with a little salt and pepper.
4. Add the wine, bring to a boil over high heat and reduce the liquids by half.
5. Add the carrot juice, bring to a boil over high heat and reduce the liquids by half.
6. Reduce the heat back to medium, add the crushed tomatoes and basil and stir. Add the remaining salt, pepper and paprika and stir.
7. Brink to a boil over medium heat, reduce the heat to low, cover and cook for 25 minutes.
8. Remove from heat. Using a drink or a stick blender, mix the chunky soup into a smooth textured soup.
9. Please blend the soup carefully. You will need to let each batch run for about 2-3 minutes to reach the desired consistency. Remove from the blender into a clean pot.
10. Once you blend all the soup, place the pot on low heat. Adjust seasoning with salt and pepper and the thickness by adding water if needed. Please note that the consistency should be such that when you dip a spoon in the soup, the soup will stick to the spoon.
11. Do not boil the soup—simply bring it to a hot temperature and serve immediately.

For the garnish:

1. Place the soup in a bowl, drizzle some NHF extra virgin olive oil, then sprinkle some basil chiffonade and serve.

Breakfast | DAY 4

Blueberry Pie Smoothie

Makes 2 Servings

Ingredients

For the coconut garnish:

2 tablespoons unsweetened coconut chips

For the smoothie:

1 (14-ounce) can light coconut milk

1 cup frozen blueberries

1 frozen banana

1/4 cup rolled oats

3 tablespoons sunflower seed butter

1 teaspoon maple syrup (or maple extract to get rid of the sugar)

1/2 teaspoon vanilla extract

1/2 teaspoon ground NHF cinnamon

1/4 teaspoon ground NHF nutmeg

Method

For the garnish:

1. Preheat oven to 350°F.
2. Place shredded coconut on a sheet tray and bake in the oven until lightly browned and fragrant, 5 minutes.

For the smoothie:

1. Place smoothie ingredients in a blender, and blend until smooth, approximately 2 minutes.
2. Use a spatula to scrape down the sides of the blender, then blend for another 30 seconds.

For the assembly:

1. Pour the smoothie into a glass.
2. Garnish with shredded coconut, and drink or eat with a spoon.

Lunch | **DAY 4**

Sweet Potato-Chickpea Patties with Sriracha-Cashew Sauce

Makes 4 Servings, or 8 Three-inch Patties

Ingredients

For the patties:

1 (15-ounce) can garbanzo beans, drained and rinsed

1 medium sweet potato, peeled

1/2 medium yellow onion

2 cloves garlic, minced

2 tablespoons parsley, finely chopped

1 teaspoon NHF kosher salt

1/2 teaspoon NHF course black pepper

1 teaspoon NHF ground cumin

1/2 teaspoon NHF smoked paprika

1 teaspoon baking powder

5 tablespoons NHF extra virgin olive oil

For the cashew-Sriracha sauce:

1/2 cup raw cashews, preferably soaked for 2-3 hours

1/4 cup water, + 1-2 tablespoons as needed for thinning

1 garlic clove

2 teaspoons nutritional yeast

1 teaspoon NHF kosher salt

1 teaspoon sriracha chili sauce, + more to taste

2 tablespoons chives, finely chopped

Method

For the patties:

1. Grate the sweet potato on the small side of a box grater and the onion on the large side of a box grater.
2. In a large bowl, mash the chickpeas with a potato masher or large fork, until they are all mashed.
3. Add the sweet potatoes and onion to the bowl and stir.
4. Add the garlic, parsley, salt, pepper, cumin and smoked paprika and baking powder. Stir to combine.
5. Heat the vegetable oil in a shallow skillet until simmering. When hot, add mixture by the 1/4 cup or large spoonful to the pan. Flatten out with the back of the spoon to form a patty.
6. Fry until golden brown on one side, 3-4 minutes. Flip over and brown, another 3-4 minutes.
7. Place on a paper towel-lined plate to cool.
8. May be made the night before.

For the cashew-Sriracha sauce:

1. Place all the ingredients in a small food processor. Blend until smooth.
2. Add more chili sauce, if desired.

For the assembly:

1. Place 2-3 patties on a plate, or in a to-go container.
2. Just before serving, place a dollop of cashew sauce on top of each patty, and sprinkle with chives.
3. If taking to go, keep the sauce separate and use as a dipping sauce.

Dinner | DAY 4

Asparagus Soup

Makes 4 Servings

Ingredients

For the soup:

2 tablespoons NHF extra-virgin olive oil

1 medium leek, white portion finely chopped

1/2 pound new potatoes, peeled and cut into tiny cubes

1 tablespoon green curry paste, or to taste

1 pound asparagus, trimmed and cut into 1/2-inch segments

1 14-ounce can full-fat coconut milk

1 1/2 teaspoons NHF kosher salt, or to taste

1 teaspoon NHF course ground black pepper, or to taste

1 1/4 cups of water, or to cover

1 lemon or lime

For the garnish:

1 tablespoon chives, chopped

1/4 cup peanuts, chopped and toasted

NHF kosher salt, as needed

Method

For the soup:

1 Place a soup pot over high heat. Once the pot is hot, add extra virgin olive oil.

2 Add the leek. Stir well and cook over high heat for 4 minutes, until translucent.

3 Add the potatoes and season with a large pinch of salt and pepper. Cook, stirring constantly, for 10 minutes or until the potatoes can be just pierced with a fork.

4 Add the green curry paste and asparagus. Add the water and coconut milk, and bring to a simmer; simmer for 2-3 minutes, until the asparagus is tender.

5 Remove from heat. Using a drink blender, mix the chunky soup into a smooth puree.

6 Please blend the soup carefully. You will need to let each batch run for about 2-3 minutes to reach a smooth consistency. Remove from the blender into a clean pot.

7 Once you blend all the soup, place the pot on low heat. Adjust seasoning with salt and pepper and the thickness by adding water if needed. Please note that the consistency should be such that when you dip a spoon in the soup, the soup will stick to the spoon.

8 Do not boil the soup—simply bring it to a hot temperature and serve immediately.

For the assembly:

1 Place the soup in a bowl; place some toasted peanuts in the center of the soup.

2 Sprinkle some chopped chives on top of the soup and serve.

Breakfast | **DAY 5**

Oatmeal Muffin Cups
Makes 12 Muffins

Ingredients

For the muffins:

1/2 cup almond butter

1 1/2 cups mashed bananas (4-5 bananas) + 1 extra banana, sliced diagonally for garnish

3 cups old-fashioned oats

1 1/2 cups plain unsweetened almond milk

1 tablespoon maple syrup

1 teaspoon vanilla extract

1/2 teaspoon NHF kosher salt

1 cup raw sliced almonds + extra for topping

NHF extra virgin olive oil, for greasing the pan

For the fruit salad:

1 peach, diced

3/4 cup blueberries

2 tablespoons finely chopped mint

Method

For the muffins:

1. Preheat oven to 375°F.
2. Grease a muffin tin using NHF extra virgin olive oil.
3. Combine all ingredients in a large bowl. Stir to combine.
4. Spoon into the muffin cups, filling them 3/4 full.
5. Top with sliced banana and a few sliced almonds.
6. Bake for 20-25 minutes, or until a skewer comes out clean.
7. Wait for the cups to cool. When cool, run a butter knife around the edges and remove from tin.
8. May be made the night before for a breakfast on the go! Store in the refrigerator for 1 week, or freezer for 3 weeks.

For the fruit salad:

1. Toss together peaches, blueberries, and mint.
2. Serve on a plate with 3 muffins.

Lunch | **DAY 5**

Lentils with Dates and Golden Pine Nuts

Makes 4 Servings

Ingredients

For the lentils:

2 tablespoons NHF extra virgin olive oil

1 medium onion, finely diced

1/2 teaspoon NHF course ground black pepper

1 teaspoon NHF allspice

1 teaspoon NHF cinnamon

1/2 teaspoon NHF paprika

1 teaspoon NHF kosher salt

Long strips of peel from 1 orange

1 cup small whole green lentils

2 1/4 cups vegetable stock

8 Medjool dates, pitted and finely diced

For the garnish:

1 tablespoon NHF olive oil

1/2 teaspoon NHF cinnamon

1/2 cup pine nuts

1/2 teaspoon NHF kosher salt, or to taste

1 tablespoon finely chopped Italian parsley

Method

For the lentils:

1. Heat the olive oil in a large pot. Add the onion and sauté until translucent, about 3 minutes.
2. Add the allspice, cinnamon, paprika, and orange peel, and cook until fragrant.
3. Add the lentils and cook, stirring constantly for 5 minutes. Add the dates and stir to break up.
4. Add the vegetable stock, and simmer with a lid on the pot for 30 minutes, or until most of the liquid has been absorbed.
5. May be made the night before.

For the garnish:

1. Heat the olive oil in a pan until simmering. Add the cinnamon and stir until fragrant.
2. Add the pine nuts and stir constantly until golden brown and fragrant.
3. Toss with the parsley.

For the assembly:

1. Ladle the lentils into 4 soup or pasta bowls to serve.
2. Sprinkle the garnish in a small pile in the center of the bowl.

Hints:

- To finely dice the dates, cut them in half vertically. Then cut each half into three slivers, and cut each sliver into four sections.
- Lentils can be simmered in the vegetable stock without the spices in a large batch. You can then portion them out and freeze for up to a month. To continue this recipe, heat lentils up in a pot with the spices, dates, and 1/4 cup water and sauté for 5 minutes, until the spices are fragrant and the dates are cooked through.

Dinner | DAY 5

Corn Soup

Makes 4 Servings

Ingredients

For the soup:

2 teaspoons NHF olive oil

1/2 yellow onion, finely diced

1 medium yellow carrot, peeled and sliced into rounds

2 cups corn, fresh or frozen

2 garlic cloves

3 cups vegetable stock

1 tablespoon fresh ginger, peeled and minced or grated on a Microplane grater

2/3 cup coconut milk

2 tablespoons fresh lime juice

1 teaspoon NHF kosher salt, or to taste

1/2 teaspoon NHF ground white pepper, or to taste

For the garnish:

1 cup corn kernels, cut off the cob from 4 ears

2 tablespoons NHF Extra virgin olive oil

1 tablespoon NHF kosher salt

1 teaspoon NHF round cumin

1 teaspoon NHF coarse ground black pepper

2 tablespoons cilantro, finely chopped

1 lime, sliced into 8 wedges

For the chili oil:

1/4 cup NHF extra virgin olive oil

1 teaspoon NHF paprika

Method

For the soup:

1. Place a soup pot over high heat. Once the pot is hot, add extra virgin olive oil.
2. Add the onion and carrot and cook over high heat for 4 minutes.
3. Add the garlic and season with some of the salt and pepper.
4. Add the corn kernels and stock, and simmer for 15 minutes.
5. Add the ginger.
6. Using a drink or a stick blender, puree half the mixture, but make sure to keep some corn kernels whole.
7. Return the soup to a clean pot and add the coconut milk. Simmer for another 3 minutes.
8. Add the fresh lime juice and salt and pepper to taste. Do not boil the soup.

For the garnish:

1. Preheat oven to 400°F.
2. Toss the corn with the oil, salt, and spices and spread out on a sheet tray.
3. Bake 15 minutes, or until lightly browned.
4. Cool on the baking sheet.
5. Garnish can be kept in an airtight container at room temperature for 4 days.

For the chili oil:

1. Place the oil and paprika in a bowl and stir to combine.

For the assembly:

1. Bring the soup to hot temp and ladle into four soup bowls.
2. Sprinkle the corn garnish in a small mount in the middle of the bowl.
3. Place two lime wedges decoratively next to the corn.
4. Drizzle a few drops of hot chili oil in a large circle around the garnish.

Hints:

- To peel ginger, use the side of a spoon and a downward scraping motion.
- To slice a lime in 8 wedges, cut the lime in quarters vertically, then cut diagonally to cut out the center pit. Then cut each quarter into halves.
- You may use frozen corn for the garnish.

Breakfast | **DAY 6**

Almond Butter and Bananas on Toast

Makes 2 Slices Toast

Ingredients

For the toast:

- **1/2** cup almond butter
- **1** slice whole grain bread, toasted
- **1** banana, thinly sliced on the diagonal
- **1/2** teaspoon NHF kosher salt
- **1/4** teaspoon NHF cinnamon

Method

For the toast:

1. Toast the bread in a toaster until light brown.
2. Spread almond butter evenly over toast.
3. Layer the slices of bananas over the toast to create a shingle pattern.
4. Sprinkle salt and cinnamon evenly over the bananas.

Lunch | **DAY 6**

Spaghetti Puttanesca

Makes 4 Servings

Ingredients

For the pasta:

1 lb whole wheat spaghetti

1 teaspoon NHF kosher salt

1 tablespo1on NHF extra virgin olive oil

For the puttanesca:

1 tablespoon NHF extra virgin olive oil

6 cloves garlic

3 tablespoons capers

1 cup black olives, about 20 olives roughly chopped

1/2 red onion, finely diced

1 14 oz can crushed or diced tomatoes, with their juices

1/2 cup Italian parsley leaves, packed

1 teaspoon NHF kosher salt, or to taste

1/2 teaspoon NHF course black pepper, or to taste

1/4 cup Italian parsley, finely chopped and divided in half

Method

For the pasta:

1. Place a pot filled with water on the stove top and bring to a boil. Place the salt into the water.
2. Put the pasta in to boil for 10 minutes, or according to the package instructions. The spaghetti should be chewy but not crunchy when it is done.
3. Drain and place into a bowl with the olive oil and toss to combine. This prevents the spaghetti from sticking to itself while you make the sauce.

For the puttanesca:

1. Place a pan with the olive oil over medium heat.
2. Once it is warm but not simmering, add the onions and cook until they are starting to soften.
3. Add the garlic, capes, olives, and a pinch of salt and pepper; stir to warm but be careful not to burn the garlic.
4. Add in the tomatoes with their juices and simmer for 10 minutes.

For the assembly:

1. Toss the noodles with the sauce and Italian parsley.
2. Using a fork or tongs, twirl the noodles onto the plate and top with reserved chopped Italian parsley.

Hints:

- Using crushed tomatoes will give you a smooth sauce; using diced tomatoes will yield a chunky sauce.

Dinner | DAY 6

Jerusalem Artichoke Soup

Makes 4 Servings

Ingredients

For the soup:

2 tablespoons NHF extra virgin olive oil

1/2 yellow onion, chopped

1 medium yellow carrot, peeled and chopped

2 stalks celery, chopped

2 garlic cloves

2 pounds Jerusalem artichokes, peeled and cut into rounds

4 cups vegetable stock

1 teaspoon NHF kosher salt, or to taste

1/2 teaspoon NHF ground white pepper, or to taste

For the garnish:

1 large beet, peeled

3 tablespoons vegetable oil

NHF kosher salt, as needed to taste

1 tablespoon Italian parsley leaves

1 tablespoon NHF lemon infused olive oil

Method

For the soup:

1. Place a soup pot over high heat. Once the pot is hot, add extra virgin olive oil.
2. Add the onion, carrot, and celery and cook over high heat for 4 minutes.
3. Add the garlic and season with some of the salt and pepper.
4. Add the Jerusalem artichokes and stock, and simmer for 25-30 minutes, or until the artichokes fall apart when pricked with a fork.
5. Using a drink or a stick blender, puree the mixture until it is completely smooth. Check that it is thick enough to coat the back of a spoon. You may need to add a bit more stock or water to thin it out.
6. Add salt and pepper to taste. Do not boil the soup.

For the garnish:

1. Slice the beet thinly on a mandolin, or use a vegetable peeler to make long strips.
2. Heat olive oil in a small shallow pan until it is simmering.
3. Place the beet strips into the olive oil and fry until barely starting to brown.
4. Using a slotted spoon or tongs, remove strips from the oil and place on a paper towel to dry. Sprinkle with salt.
5. Place the lemon olive oil and parsley in a small food processor, and blend until smooth. Use a fine mesh strainer to strain out the parsley leaves. You should have a green parsley oil.

For the assembly:

1 Set out 4 soup bowls. Ladle the soup into the bowls.
2 Top with beet chips and drizzle parsley oil around the soup.

Hints:

- To peel Jerusalem artichokes, use the side of a spoon and a downward scraping motion.
- If you cannot find Jerusalem artichokes, you may substitute parsnips (they look like white carrots). Peel them, cut them into rounds, and substitute directly for the artichokes. They have the same cook time.

Breakfast | DAY 7

Almond Apple, Almond, and Date Breakfast Charoset

Makes 4 Servings

Ingredients

For the charoset:

1 granny smith apple, peeled and finely diced

2/3 cup whole almonds, toasted and finely chopped

6 whole dates, finely diced

1 teaspoon NHF ground cinnamon

1/2 teaspoon NHF kosher salt

1/4 cup fresh squeezed orange juice

2 tablespoons nonalcoholic red wine or grape juice

1/2 a lemon, juiced

For the assembly:

1/4 cup soy or coconut based plain unsweetened yogurt

Method

For the charoset:

1. Mix together the apples, almonds, dates, cinnamon, cardamom, and salt.
2. Pour on the orange juice, wine, and lemon juice, and stir to combine.

For the assembly:

1. Spoon into breakfast bowls.
2. Top with a dollop of plain yogurt.

Hints:

- To finely dice the dates, cut them in half vertically. Then cut each half into three slivers, and cut each sliver into four sections.

Lunch | DAY 7

Farro Salad with Butternut Squash and Roasted Red Onions

Makes 4 Servings

Ingredients

For the farro salad:

1 cup farro, rinsed and drained

1 teaspoon NHF kosher salt

2 1/2 cups vegetable stock

Juice of half a lemon

For the squash:

1 1/2 cups butternut squash, peeled and cut into 1/2 -inch dice

1/2 large red onion, cut into 1/2 inch thick slivers

2 teaspoons fresh thyme, minced

1 teaspoon fresh sage, minced

2 teaspoons NHF za'atar

1 tablespoon NHF extra virgin olive oil

1 teaspoon NHF balsamic vinegar

For the garnish:

3 tablespoons NHF extra virgin olive oil

1/4 cup walnuts, deeply toasted

1/2 cup baby arugula

Method

For the farro:

1. Heat the olive oil in a large pot until simmering. Add the farro and stir until toasted and fragrant, about 2 minutes.

2. Add the salt, stock, and lemon juice and bring to a boil. Cover the pot and turn the heat down to low. Simmer for 15 minutes.

3. Remove from heat and let sit for 5 minutes. Fluff with a fork.

For the squash and onions:

1. Preheat the oven to 400°F.

2. Toss the squash, onions, thyme, sage, Za'atar, salt, and olive oil together. Spread on a rimmed sheet pan covered with foil.

3. Roast for 20 minutes, stirring every 5, or until the squash is tender when pierced with a fork.

For the assembly:

1. In a large bowl, toss together the farro, squash and onion mixture. This mixture may be kept in the refrigerator for up to a week and eaten hot or cold.

2. To serve, place in a shallow pasta bowl and top with toasted walnuts and micro greens. Drizzle with walnut oil.

Hints:

- Farro can be substituted with brown rice and cooked per package instructions.

Dinner | **DAY 7**

Black Bean Soup with Cilantro Cashew Cream Sauce

Makes 4 Servings

Ingredients

For the black beans:

1 pound black beans, rinsed and picked over

1 medium yellow onion, peeled and quartered

4 cloves garlic, smashed

1 teaspoon NHF ground cloves

1 gallon water

2 tablespoons NHF kosher salt

1 tablespoon NHF red wine vinegar

For the soup:

2 tablespoons NHF extra virgin olive oil

1/2 yellow onion, chopped

2 medium carrots, peeled and cut into half moons

2 stalks celery, chopped

1 medium zucchini, cut into half moons

1 cup cherry tomatoes, halved

2 garlic cloves

1 tablespoon NHF ground cumin

2 teaspoons NHF paprika

2 cups cooked black beans

4 cups vegetable stock

1 teaspoon NHF kosher salt, or to taste

1/2 teaspoon NHF course black pepper, or to taste

For the cilantro cashew cream sauce:

1/2 cup cashews

1/4 cup water

Juice of 1/2 lime

1 teaspoon NHF cider vinegar

1 garlic clove, minced

1/4 cup cilantro leaves

1 teaspoon NHF kosher salt

Method

For the black beans:

1. Place the beans in a colander in the sink and rinse to get rid of any dirt. Pick out any rocks or twigs that you might see as well.

2. Transfer the beans to a large pot and cover with four inches of cold water. Let soak overnight or up to 24 hours.

3. Drain and rinse the beans in a colander, and return to the pot. Add the onion, garlic, garlic cloves, and water.

4. Place over medium-high heat until the water comes to a boil. Reduce the heat to medium-low to keep it at a simmer.

5. Simmer for 30-40 minutes, or until the beans are soft but not falling apart. Remove from heat and stir in salt and red wine vinegar. Cool completely, then portion into 2 cup pint containers. Containers may be frozen for up to a month.

For the soup:

1. Heat the oil in a large-bottomed pot. Add the onions and sauté until translucent, 4 minutes.
2. Add the carrot, celery, zucchini, tomatoes, garlic, cumin, and paprika, and sauté another 4 minutes.
3. Add the black beans and stock, and bring to a boil. Cook for 5 minutes, until the carrots are tender when pierced with a fork.
4. Using a drink or a stick blender, puree the mixture until it is completely smooth. Check that it is thick enough to coat the back of a spoon. You may need to add a bit more stock or water to thin it out.
5. Season with salt and pepper to taste.

For the cilantro cashew cream:

1. Soak the cashews in water for 1 hour (may be done the day before, or skipped if pressed for time)
2. Place the cashews, water, lime, vinegar, garlic, 3/4 of the cilantro, and salt in a blender and blend until completely smooth.

For the assembly:

1. Set out 4 soup bowls. Ladle the soup into the bowls.
2. Top with a dollop of cilantro cashew cream, and place a few remaining cilantro leaves decoratively on top.

Hints:

- Cook a large pot of black beans at the beginning of the month and freeze in small containers for faster meals.
- You may substitute canned black beans to save time.

Breakfast | **DAY 8**

Orzo Salad with Broccoli, Tomatoes, and Olives

Makes 4 Servings

Ingredients

For the orzo:

1 1/2 cup whole wheat orzo

1 teaspoon NHF kosher salt

1 tablespoon NHF extra virgin olive oil

For the vegetables:

1 small head broccoli, cut into small florets

1 cup cherry tomatoes, sliced in half

1 bunch basil, sliced into long slivers "chiffonade"

1/2 cup Kalamata olives, thinly sliced but leave 4 whole for garnish

For the vinaigrette:

1 tablespoons NHF extra virgin olive oil

1/3 cup NHF white wine vinegar

1/2 teaspoon NHF kosher salt

1 tablespoon honey

Method

For the orzo:

1. Bring a large pot of water with a teaspoon of salt to boil over medium heat.

2. Add the orzo and cook for 10 minutes, stirring occasionally to make sure it doesn't stick together. It is done when it has a firm, chewy texture.

3. Drain the water and, in a medium bowl, toss the orzo with 1 tablespoon olive oil and 1 teaspoon salt.

For the vegetables:

1. Bring a large pot of water with a teaspoon of salt to boil over medium heat.

2. Prepare a large bowl of half ice, half water and place in the sink.

3. Using a strainer, place the broccoli florets into the boiling water for 30 seconds, until they turn bright green.

4. Remove with the strainer and immediately plunge the strainer into the ice water bath in the sink.

5. Drain the broccoli once it is cold and toss with the tomatoes, olives, and most of the basil.

For the vinaigrette:

1. In a medium sized bowl, whisk all ingredients with a fork until well combined and smooth.

For the assembly:

1. Toss together the orzo, vegetables, and vinaigrette to evenly coat.

2. Place a heaping cup full mounded on to the center of each plate so that you can see some of each type of vegetable.

3. Top with the remaining basil chiffonade and a whole olive.

Hints:

- To chiffonade basil, stack 5 leaves on top of each other and roll up into a tight cylinder. Finely slice the length of the roll to make long slivers.

Lunch | **DAY 8**

White Bean and Pepper Salad

Makes 4 Servings

Ingredients

For the white beans:

1 pound dry white beans

1 medium onion, quartered

2 garlic cloves, smashed

10 cups water

2 tablespoons NHF kosher salt

2 teaspoons NHF cider vinegar

For the red pepper:

2 red peppers

For the vinaigrette:

1/4 cup NHF red wine vinegar

1 tablespoon Dijon mustard

1 teaspoon honey

1/2 cup NHF extra virgin olive oil

1/2 teaspoon NHF kosher salt

For the assembly:

1/2 cup finely chopped Italian parsley

2 roasted red peppers, finely diced

1/2 red onion, finely diced

Method

For the white beans:

1. Place the beans in a colander in the sink and rinse to get rid of any dirt. Pick out any rocks or twigs that you might see as well.

2. Transfer the beans to a large pot and cover with four inches of cold water. Let soak overnight or up to 24 hours.

3. Drain and rinse the beans in a colander, and return to the pot. Add the onion, garlic, bay leaves, and water.

4. Place over medium-high heat until the water comes to a boil. Reduce the heat to medium-low to keep it at a simmer.

5. Simmer for 30-40 minutes, or until the beans are soft but not falling apart. Remove from heat and stir in salt and cider vinegar. Cool completely, then portion into 2 cup pint containers. Containers may be frozen for up to a month.

For the red pepper:

1. Place the pepper directly on the flame of a burner turned to high heat.

2. Once one side is fully blackened, use metal tongs to turn slightly. Keep rotating the pepper until all sides are fully blackened.

3. Once it is fully blackened, place in a large bowl and cover with plastic wrap. Let it sit for 5 minutes to loosen the skin.

4. Gently rub the blackened skin off the red pepper.

5. Slice into thin slices. May be kept in the fridge for up to 3 days.

For the vinaigrette:

1. In a medium sized bowl, whisk all ingredients with a fork until well combined and smooth.

For the assembly:

1. Toss together the white beans, red peppers, onion, parsley, and vinaigrette.
2. Spoon into pasta bowls or containers.
3. Place a whole parsley leaf on top to garnish.

Hints:

- To chiffonade basil, stack the leaves on top of each other and roll into a cigar shape. Then finely slice the cigar into small strips.

- You may use canned white beans, also called cannellini beans. Use two 14-oz cans for this recipe.

Dinner | **DAY 8**

Mixed Mushroom Soup with Truffled Cashew Crema

Makes 4 Servings

Ingredients

For the soup:

2 teaspoons NHF extra virgin olive oil

3/4 pound oyster mushrooms, finely chopped

1/4 pound shiitake, finely chopped

1 yellow onion, diced

3 garlic cloves, finely minced

1/2 cup white wine

4 cups vegetable stock

2 tablespoons corn starch

2 tablespoons water

10 sprigs of thyme, leaves stripped off

1 teaspoon NHF kosher salt, or to taste

1/2 teaspoon NHF ground white pepper, or to taste

1/2 cup cashew crème fraiche

For the cashew crème fraiche:

1/2 cup raw cashews

3 tablespoons raw slivered almonds (must be peeled)

1/4 cup lemon juice (from approximately 2 small lemons)

1/2 cup water

1 tablespoon NHF apple cider vinegar

1 tablespoon nutritional yeast

1 teaspoon NHF kosher salt

For the garnish:

1 cup shiitake mushrooms, chopped

1 tablespoon NHF extra virgin olive oil

1 teaspoon NHF kosher salt

1 small bunch chives, finely chopped

1/4 cup Italian parsley leaves, finely chopped but leave out a small handful for plating

1/2 teaspoon NHF truffle oil, or to taste

1/2 teaspoon cracked black pepper

Method

For the soup:

1. Place a soup pot over high heat. Once the pot is hot, add extra virgin olive oil.

2. Add the onion and sauté for 4 minutes, until translucent. Add the garlic and sauté for another 2 minutes. Remove from pot and place in a large mixing bowl.

3. Working in batches, place a single layer of mushrooms in 1 tablespoon of oil and brown. Do not stir as it will prevent the mushrooms from browning. Remove from the pot and place in a mixing bowl. You may need to do 2-3 batches to brown all the mushrooms.

4. Put all the mushrooms and onion and garlic mixture back in the pot and deglaze the pan with 1/2 cup white wine. Scrape the bottom of the pan with a wooden spoon to get all the browned bits incorporated into the wine.

For the cashew crème fraiche:

1. Soak the cashews and almonds overnight, or a minimum of 2-3 hours.
2. Drain and rinse well and put in a blender.
3. Add in the rest of the ingredients and blend until smooth. You may need to stop the blender once or twice and use a spatula to scrape down the sides to incorporate all the ingredients.
4. May be stored in the fridge up to 10 days.

For the mushroom garnish:

1. Set a medium sauté pan on medium heat. Add 1 tablespoon olive oil to the pan.
2. When the oil is simmering, add the mushrooms and brown on one side. Stir until evenly cooked and browned all over and remove from heat.
3. Toss with chopped chives and parsley.

For the assembly:

1. Set out 4 soup bowls. Ladle the soup into the bowls.
2. Place 2 tablespoons of mushroom garnish in the middle of the bowl.
3. Drizzle truffle oil around the edges; sprinkle with cracked pepper.
4. Garnish with a whole leaf of Italian parsley placed on top of the mushrooms.

Breakfast | DAY 9

Shakshuka with Sweet Potatoes

Makes 4 Servings

Ingredients

For the sweet potatoes:

2 small sweet potatoes, peeled and sliced into tin rounds (8-10 total)

1 teaspoon NHF kosher salt

2 teaspoons NHF extra virgin olive oil

For the shakshuka sauce:

2 tablespoons NHF extra virgin olive oil

1/2 yellow onion, finely diced

2 red peppers, finely diced

2 teaspoons tomato paste

2 teaspoons NHF granulated garlic

2 tablespoons NHF ground cumin

1 tablespoon NHF smoked paprika

1 15-oz can no-salt added diced tomatoes

1 tablespoon NHF apple cider vinegar

1 teaspoon NHF kosher salt, or to taste

1/2 teaspoon NHF course ground black pepper, or to taste

1/4 cup Italian parsley, finely chopped

Method

For the sweet potatoes:

1. Preheat the oven to 375°F.
2. Place the sliced sweet potatoes on a sheet pan and drizzle with olive oil and a pinch of salt.
3. Roast in the oven until starting to brown and tender when pierced with a fork, about 10 minutes.

For the shakshuka sauce:

1. Preheat the oven to 375°F.
2. Place a medium sized pot over medium-high heat and place the olive oil in the pan.
3. Place the diced onion and peppers in the hot oil and sauté for 4 minutes, until fragrant and translucent.
4. Add the tomato paste, granulated garlic, cumin and smoked paprika and stir until the spices are fragrant, about 2 more minutes.
5. Add the diced tomatoes, cider vinegar, salt, and pepper. Turn down the heat and cook for 15 minutes, until the tomatoes start to fall apart.
6. Transfer the sauce to a 10" cast iron pan or 8x8 baking dish, or 8 ramekins for individual servings.
7. Nestle the sweet potatoes into the sauce. Make sure the potatoes are still visible on top and that you can see sauce surrounding them.
8. Bake in the oven for 10-15 minutes, or until the sweet potatoes are tender when pierced with a fork.
9. Sprinkle parsley on top and serve family-style at the table, or serve individual ramekins.

Hints:

- To prepare this meal for the coming days, make the sauce and place in pint containers. May be refrigerated for 3 days or frozen up to 1 month. When ready to eat, defrost the sauce and bake with the sweet potatoes on top.

- To save time, you may also roast the rounds of sweet potatoes in the oven on a sheet tray with 1 tablespoon of olive oil and 1/2 teaspoon of salt sprinkled over while the sauce is cooking on the stove. Transfer sauce to serving dish, and place potatoes on top.

Lunch | **DAY 9**

Grilled Leeks with Romesco Sauce

Makes 4 Servings

Ingredients

For the romesco sauce:

1/4 cup NHF extra virgin olive oil

1 red pepper, finely diced

1 teaspoon NHF granulated garlic

1/2 teaspoon NHF paprika

1 14 oz can diced tomatoes, drained and juice saved for rice

1 slice whole wheat bread, torn into pieces

2 teaspoons NHF white wine vinegar

3/4 cup blanched almonds, toasted to medium brown

2 tablespoons hazelnuts, toasted and peeled

1 teaspoon NHF coarse ground black pepper

2 teaspoons NHF kosher salt

For the leeks:

4 medium to large leeks, sliced in half lengthwise and cleaned

4 teaspoons NHF extra virgin olive oil

1 teaspoon NHF kosher salt

For the marinade:

1/2 cup NHF extra virgin olive oil

1/4 cup NHF balsamic vinegar

1 teaspoon honey

1 teaspoon Dijon mustard

1 garlic clove, minced

1/2 teaspoon NHF kosher salt

1/4 teaspoon NHF course ground black pepper

For the rice:

1 cup long grain brown rice

Juice from can of diced tomatoes in the romesco sauce

2 teaspoons NHF extra virgin olive oil

2 cups water

1 teaspoon NHF kosher salt

Method

For the romesco sauce:

1. Place all the ingredients in a blender or food processor.

2. If it is too thick to blend into a smooth puree, add olive oil or water 1 tablespoon at a time until it is completely smooth.

For the leeks:

1. Bring a large pot of water to a boil.

2. Place the leeks in the water for 30 seconds each, and remove from water with tongs. Only do 1 leek at a time. Immediately place the leeks in an ice bath. (To make an ice bath, fill a bowl halfway with ice, and put in enough water to cover. There should be a lot of ice!)

3. Brush the leeks with olive oil on both sides and place in the marinade.

For the marinade:

1. Place all ingredients in a jar and shake vigorously to combine.

For the grilling:

1. Heat a grill to medium-high. It is ready when you sprinkle water on it and the water immediately sizzles.
2. Brush the grill with vegetable oil.
3. Place the leeks on the grill cut side down until charred, about 5 minutes. Brush with marinade.
4. Turn over and char the back side, another 4-5 minutes. Brush with marinade one more time.
5. Repeat with remaining leeks.

For the rice:

1. Rinse the rice in a strainer.
2. Heat olive oil in a 2 quart saucepan. When simmering, add the rice and stir constantly until fragrant and lightly toasted.
3. Pour in the water and tomato juice and bring to a boil. Once it reaches a boil, turn the heat down to low until it is simmering. Put a lid on it.
4. Cook for 30-35 minutes, or until all the liquid is absorbed.
5. Check to make sure it is cooked all the way. It should be chewy and not crunchy. If it is crunchy, add more water and put back on the heat. If it is done and there is still water, drain the water in a colander and put the rice back in the pot.
6. Remove rice from heat and let sit with the lid on for an additional 10 minutes. Fluff with a fork.

For the assembly:

1. Evenly divide the rice and place each portion in a small bowl. Pack it in and turn the bowl out onto a plate.
2. Place 2 leeks on top of the rice and dollop with romesco sauce and sprinkle with salt.

Hints:

- To clean the leeks, cut in half lengthwise, and run under cold water, fanning the layers out, but keeping the whole vegetable in tact.
- Romesco sauce may be made up to 3 days ahead of time and kept refrigerated.
- To peel hazelnuts, toast, and then while still hot, place in a clean dish towel and rub between your fingers to get the husks off.
- Romesco sauce can be made with only almonds or only hazelnuts, if you so desire.
- Adding the juice from canned tomatoes is a great way to add flavor to any grain you are cooking.
- If you use olive oil on the grill, it will smoke a lot. Use a high smoke point oil like canola, safflower, or grape seed.

Dinner | **DAY 9**

Carrot, Spinach, and Dill Soup

Makes 4 Servings

Ingredients

For the soup:

2 tablespoons NHF extra virgin olive oil

1 yellow onion, chopped

6 medium yellow carrots, peeled and chopped

2 stalks celery, chopped

2 garlic cloves, minced

1 teaspoon NHF ground turmeric

1 pound spinach, fresh or frozen

2 tablespoons dill leaves, packed

4 cups vegetable stock

1 teaspoon NHF kosher salt, or to taste

1/2 teaspoon NHF ground white pepper, or to taste

For the garnish:

1 large carrot, peeled

3 tablespoons extra virgin olive oil

NHF kosher salt

2 tablespoons dill leaves

1 tablespoon NHF lemon infused olive oil

Method

For the soup:

1. Place a soup pot over high heat. Once the pot is hot, add extra virgin olive oil.

2. Add the onion, carrot, and celery and cook over high heat for 4 minutes.

3. Add the garlic and turmeric and season with some of the salt and pepper.

4. Add the stock, and simmer for 15-20 minutes or until the carrots fall apart when pricked with a fork.

5. Add in the spinach and dill.

6. Using a drink blender, puree the mixture until it is completely smooth. Check that it is thick enough to coat the back of a spoon. You may need to add a bit more stock or water to thin it out.

7. Add salt and pepper to taste. Do not boil the soup after the spinach is added or it will turn brown.

For the garnish:

1. Slice the carrot into rounds thinly on a mandolin, or use a vegetable peeler to make long strips.

2. Heat extra virgin olive oil in a small shallow pan until it is simmering.

3. Place the carrot coins or strips into the olive oil and fry until barely starting to brown.

4. Using a slotted spoon or tongs, remove strips from the oil and place on a paper towel to dry. Sprinkle with salt.

5. Place the lemon oil and dill in a small food processor or blender, and blend until smooth. Use a fine mesh strainer to strain it. You should have green dill oil.

For the assembly:

1. Set out 4 soup bowls. Ladle the soup into the bowls.

2. Top with carrot chips and drizzle dill oil around the soup.

Breakfast | **DAY 10**

Kale and Sweet Potato Breakfast Burrito

Makes 4 Servings

Ingredients

For the burrito:

1 medium sweet potato, peeled and diced

1/4 cup NHF extra virgin olive oil

1 teaspoon NHF kosher salt

1/2 cup quinoa, cooked

1/2 cup lentils, cooked

2 cups Tuscan kale, stems removed and leaves sliced thinly

Juice of 1/2 lemon

1 tablespoon NHF balsamic vinegar

2 teaspoons fresh thyme, finely chopped

1 teaspoon NHF kosher salt

1 medium tomato, diced

1 small cucumber, diced

1 small avocado, diced

4 brown rice or whole wheat tortillas

For the hummus:

1 can chickpeas, drained approx 1 cup

2 tablespoons water

1 clove garlic

2 teaspoons NHF kosher salt, or to taste

1/4 cup tahini

Juice from 1 lemon

1 teaspoon NHF cumin

1/2 teaspoon NHF paprika

2 tablespoons NHF olive oil

Method

For the burrito:

1. Preheat the oven to 400°F.
2. Toss the sweet potatoes with the olive oil and large pinch of salt. Spread out on a sheet tray.
3. Bake in the oven for 10 minutes, or until lightly browned and tender when pierced with a fork.
4. In a medium bowl, rub the remaining olive oil on the kale and then toss with salt and lemon juice.
5. Mix the remaining ingredients except the avocado in a large bowl, fluffing with a fork. This may be done up to 3 days in advance. Add the avocado before assembling to prevent it from turning brown.

For the hummus:

1. Put the chickpeas, garlic, salt, cumin, paprika, tahini, and water in a blender and turn on low. With the blender running, slowly drizzle in the olive oil.
2. Blend until smooth, adding more olive oil as needed to thin out the hummus and create a completely smooth texture. Taste for salt and add more if needed.
3. May be made in advance. Will keep in the refrigerator up to one week.

For the assembly:

1. Lay out a tortilla and spread with hummus.
2. Spoon grain and sweet potato mixture on top.
3. Roll up and slice in half.

Hints:

- You may use store-bought hummus if you are pressed for time.

Lunch | **DAY 10**

Baked Red Lentil Falafel Salad with Artichoke Bruschetta

Makes 4 Servings

Ingredients

For the falafel:

1/2 cup dry split red lentils, soaked overnight in cold water

1 cup cilantro leaves, cleaned and picked off the stem

1 cup Italian parsley leaves, cleaned and picked off the stem

1/2 medium red onion, diced

3 cloves garlic, minced

3 teaspoons tahini paste

3 teaspoons NHF extra virgin olive oil

1 teaspoon NHF kosher salt

1/2 teaspoon NHF course ground black pepper

1/2 teaspoon NHF ground cumin

1/4 teaspoon baking soda

2 tablespoons whole wheat flour, or chickpea flour if gluten free

For the salad:

1 medium head gem lettuce or Boston bibb lettuce, torn into pieces

1 yellow bell pepper, sliced into 1/4 inch thick sections

1 small carrot, julienned

3 tablespoons NHF extra virgin olive oil

Juice of half a lemon

1/2 teaspoon NHF kosher salt

For the artichoke bruschetta:

1 jar baby artichokes or 1 cup frozen, cut into small dices and defrosted

4 garlic cloves, smashed

2 teaspoons NHF extra virgin olive oil

1 teaspoon NHF kosher salt

1 lemon, cut in half

1/2 cup mint leaves, picked and finely chopped

Method

For the patties:

1. Preheat the oven to 375°F.

2. Drain the lentils. Place the soaked lentils in the bowl of a food processor along with the cilantro, parsley, onion, and garlic. Pulse 5 times.

3. Add the tahini paste, olive oil, salt, pepper and spices. Pulse another few times until almost smooth but still crumbly.

4. Add the baking soda and flour and pulse to combine.

5. Refrigerate for 30 minutes, up to overnight. May be made the night before.

6. Using wet hands, form the mixture into balls and place on a piece of parchment paper on a baking sheet or in a 9x13 pan. You should get 10-12 falafel balls.

7. Bake for 15-18 minutes, or until lightly browned. Do not over bake!

For the artichoke bruschetta:

1. Heat olive oil in a pan. Add the diced artichokes and brown on one side.

2. Turn off the heat, add the chopped garlic to the pan and toss to combine.

3. Add the lemon juice and chopped mint and season with salt and pepper.

For the salad assembly:

1. Toss the lettuce with the olive oil, lemon juice, salt, carrots and peppers.

2. Spoon the artichokes on top and toss to combine.

3. Place falafel on top.

4. If taking to go, toss the lettuce with carrot and peppers. Toss with artichoke, lemon, and olive oil just before eating.

Dinner | **DAY 10**

Yellow Lentil Soup (Dal)

Makes 4 Servings

Ingredients

For the soup:

2 tablespoons NHF extra virgin olive oil

1 medium onion, finely diced

1/2 teaspoon NHF course ground black pepper

1 teaspoon NHF kosher salt

1 teaspoon NHF ground turmeric

1 teaspoon NHF paprika masala

1 teaspoon NHF cumin

2 cloves garlic, minced

1/2 cup tomatoes, diced from half a can or 2 small fresh

1/2 inch ginger, grated on the small side of a box grater, or a Microplane

1 cup yellow or red split peas

2 1/4 cups vegetable stock or water

For the garnish:

2 tablespoons cilantro leaves

Method

For the soup:

1. Heat the olive oil in a large pot. Add the onion and sauté until translucent, about 3 minutes.
2. Add the turmeric and garam masala and cook until fragrant.
3. Add the garlic, ginger, and lentils, and stir to combine.
4. Add the vegetable stock, and simmer for 15-20 minutes, stirring every now and then. If it doesn't look soupy enough, add more water to thin out.
5. Taste for salt and pepper.
6. May be made the night before.

For the garnish:

1. Ladle the lentils into four soup or pasta bowls to serve.
2. Place a few cilantro leaves off-center in the bowl.
3. You may serve with store-bought whole wheat naan.

Breakfast | **DAY 11**

Green Smoothie

Makes 2 Servings

Ingredients

For the smoothie:

3 cups Tuscan kale, stems removed and leaves sliced thinly

16 oz coconut water

1/2 lemon, zested and juiced

1 cup frozen mango

1 small granny smith apple, diced

1 small cucumber, or half of a large one

1 rib celery

Method

For the smoothie:

1. Place all the ingredients in a blender and blend until smooth. Add more coconut water if it isn't smooth enough. The smoothie should be thick enough to coat the back of a spoon, and there should be no chunks in it.

2. Pour into a glass and enjoy!

Lunch | **DAY 11**

Kale Salad with Apricots, Avocado, and Almonds

Makes 4 Servings

Ingredients

For the salad:

4 cups Tuscan kale, leaves torn and stems removed

2 tablespoons NHF extra virgin olive oil

1 teaspoon NHF kosher salt

1/2 cup dried apricots, sliced

1 small avocado, diced

1/2 red onion, thinly sliced

1 cup slivered almonds, toasted

1/2 cup cannellini beans

For the dressing:

3 tablespoons NHF red wine vinegar

2 teaspoons Dijon mustard

1 teaspoon honey

1/3 cup NHF extra virgin olive oil

1/2 teaspoon NHF kosher salt

1/2 orange, juiced

Method

For the salad:

1. Place the kale and olive oil in a large mixing bowl and massage the oil into the kale.

2. Place other ingredients in the bowl and toss to combine.

3. If making the evening before, omit the avocado.

For the dressing:

1. Place all ingredients in a jar and shake vigorously to combine. You might need to scrape the honey or mustard off the side of the jar and shake again.

For the assembly:

1. Pour the dressing over the salad and toss to combine.

2. Let sit 15-20 minutes before eating.

Dinner | **DAY 11**

Minestrone Soup

Makes 4 Servings

Ingredients

For the soup:

2 tablespoons NHF extra virgin olive oil

1/2 yellow onion, diced

1 medium yellow carrot, peeled and diced

2 stalks celery, diced

1 cup diced zucchini

2 garlic cloves

2 tablespoons tomato paste

3 teaspoons NHF Italian seasoning

1 teaspoon NHF kosher salt, or to taste

1/2 teaspoon NHF course ground black pepper, or to taste

1 can diced tomatoes

1 can kidney beans, rinsed and drained

3 cups vegetable stock

1 cup quinoa pasta, optional

1 cup frozen spinach

For the garnish:

1 small bunch Italian parsley, finely chopped

Method

For the soup:

1. Place a soup pot over high heat. Once the pot is hot, add extra virgin olive oil.
2. Add the onion, carrot, celery, Italian seasoning, and red pepper flakes, and cook over high heat for 4 minutes, until the onions are soft.
3. Add the garlic and season with some of the salt and pepper.
4. Add tomatoes with their juices, stock, pasta (if using), and zucchini, and simmer for 15 minutes.
5. Add in the frozen spinach and cook just until heated through.
6. Adjust seasoning with salt and pepper.

For the assembly:

1. Set out 4 soup bowls. Ladle the soup into the bowls.
2. Sprinkle Italian parsley over the center of the soup.

Breakfast | **DAY 12**

Black Rice Pudding

Makes 4 Servings

Ingredients

For the pudding:

1 cup black rice

2 1/2 cups water

1 14 oz can coconut milk

2 tablespoons honey

1/4 teaspoon NHF kosher salt

For the garnish:

1/2 cup unsweetened coconut chips, toasted

1/2 mango, diced

Method

For the pudding:

1. Place the rice, coconut milk, and water in a pot on the stove.
2. Simmer for 40 minutes, stirring every few minutes until the rice is soft and cooked through. If it gets dry, add water 1/4 cup at a time. The rice should be soft and chewy, and not crunchy when it is cooked through.
3. Stir in the honey and salt to taste. Can be made the night before and reheated or eaten cold.

For the assembly:

1. Spoon the pudding into a bowl.
2. Top with toasted coconut chips and diced mango.

Hints:

- If you are rushed for time, you may use basmati rice and reduce the cook time to 20 minutes.
- When reheating, stir in 2 tablespoons of water or coconut milk to thin out consistency.

Lunch | **DAY 12**

Shepherd's Pie

Makes 4 Servings

Ingredients

For the lentils:

2 tablespoons NHF extra virgin olive oil

1 medium onion, finely diced

2 cloves garlic

1 tablespoon fresh thyme, finely chopped

1/2 teaspoon NHF coarse ground black pepper

1 teaspoon NHF kosher salt

1 1/2 cups whole green or brown lentils

4 cups vegetable stock

1/2 cup peas, fresh or frozen

1/2 cup corn kernels, fresh or frozen

1 medium carrot, peeled and diced

For the potatoes:

3 lbs potatoes, peeled and diced

1/4 cup NHF extra virgin olive oil

1 teaspoon nutritional yeast

1/2 teaspoon NHF coarse ground black pepper

1 teaspoon NHF kosher salt

1/4 cup Italian parsley, finely chopped

Method

For the lentils:

1. Heat the olive oil in a large pot. Add the onion and sauté until translucent, about 4 minutes.
2. Add the garlic, lentils, carrot and a pinch each of salt and pepper. Stir to soften the carrots, around 2 minutes.
3. Add the stock and simmer with the lid on for 20 minutes, or until the lentils are tender.
4. Stir in the peas and corn kernels.

For the potatoes:

1. Boil the potatoes with a large pinch of salt in enough water to cover them by 2 inches or more.
2. When they can be easily pierced with a fork, drain the water. Return to the pot and add the olive oil and nutritional yeast.
3. Mash with a potato masher until mostly creamy. Add a small amount of water if you need more liquid.
4. Toss with the parsley.

For the assembly:

1. Preheat oven to 400°F.
2. Ladle the lentils into an 8x8-inch baking pan or 9-inch pie tin.
3. Place spoonfuls of the potato mixture on top and spread out to create a uniform topping.
4. Bake for 10 minutes, or until the top starts to brown.
5. Sprinkle Italian parsley over the top.

Dinner | **DAY 12**

Broccoli Soup

Makes 4 Servings

Ingredients

For the soup:

2 tablespoons NHF extra virgin olive oil

1 large yellow onion, diced

1 medium yellow carrot, peeled and diced

2 stalks celery, diced

2 garlic cloves

2 heads of broccoli, chopped

4 cups vegetable stock

1 teaspoon NHF kosher salt, or to taste

1/2 teaspoon NHF course ground black pepper, or to taste

For the garnish:

1/2 cup slivered almonds

1 tablespoon NHF extra virgin olive oil

1 teaspoon chopped thyme

1/2 teaspoon NHF kosher salt

Method

For the soup:

1. Place a soup pot over high heat. Once the pot is hot, add extra virgin olive oil.
2. Add the onion, carrot, and celery and cook over high heat for 4 minutes.
3. Add the garlic and season with some of the salt and pepper.
4. Add the broccoli and stock, and simmer for 15-20 minutes, or until the broccoli is tender when pricked with a fork.
5. Using a drink or a stick blender, puree the mixture until it is completely smooth. Check that it is thick enough to coat the back of a spoon. You may need to add a bit more stock or water to thin the mixture out.
6. Add salt and pepper to taste. Do not boil the soup—gently warm it to the desired temperature.

For the assembly:

1. Place the olive oil in a small pan over high heat.
2. Add the almonds and stir until lightly toasted and fragrant.
3. Toss with the salt and thyme.

For the assembly:

1. Set out 4 soup bowls. Ladle the soup into the bowls.
2. Top with almonds.

Breakfast | **DAY 13**

Vanilla and Cinnamon Quinoa Pudding

Makes 4 Servings

Ingredients

For the pudding:

1 cup quinoa, rinsed

2 1/2 cups water

1 14 oz can coconut milk

2 teaspoons NHF ground cinnamon

1 teaspoon NHF ground cloves

2 teaspoons vanilla extract

2 tablespoons honey

1/4 teaspoon NHF kosher salt

For the garnish:

1/2 cup pistachios, toasted

1/2 cup raspberries, rinsed

Method

For the pudding:

1. Place the quinoa, coconut milk, and water in a pot on the stove. Stir in the honey, cinnamon, cloves, salt, and vanilla to dissolve.

2. Simmer for 30 minutes, stirring every few minutes until the quinoa is soft and cooked through. If it gets dry, add water 1/4 cup at a time.

3. Can be made the night before and reheated or eaten cold.

For the assembly:

1. Spoon the pudding into a bowl.

2. Top with pistachios and raspberries.

Lunch | **DAY 13**

Marinated Grilled Vegetables with Orange Cilantro Marinade

Makes 4 Servings

Ingredients

For the grilled vegetables:

1 zucchini, cut in 1/4 inch ribbons lengthwise

1 yellow squash, cut in 1/4 inch ribbons lengthwise

1 Japanese eggplant, cut in 1/4 inch ribbons lengthwise

2 portabello mushrooms, sliced 1/4 inch thick

1 large red onion, sliced 1/2 inch thick

1 red pepper, cut into 1/2 inch vertical strips

1 teaspoon NHF kosher salt

For the marinade:

1/2 cup NHF extra virgin olive oil

1 teaspoon NHF red wine vinegar

1 teaspoon Dijon mustard

1/4 cup orange juice, squeezed from 2 oranges

2 tablespoons cilantro leaves, finely chopped

For the assembly:

1/4 cup walnuts, deeply toasted

Method

For the marinade:

1. Place all the ingredients in a jar and shake to combine.

For the grilled vegetables:

1. Place all the vegetables in a shallow baking pan, sprinkle salt over, and cover with marinade. Let sit for a minimum of 15 minutes, up to overnight.
2. Heat the grill or grill pan.
3. Working in batches, place a single layer of vegetables on the grill, and grill until dark grill marks are visible, approx. 3-4 minutes.
4. Turn over and grill another 3-4 minutes.
5. Transfer to a clean platter. Repeat with remaining vegetables.

For the assembly:

1. Arrange the vegetables overlapping on a platter. Drizzle with some of the leftover vinaigrette.
2. Sprinkle toasted walnuts over the top.

Hints:

- You may use any vegetables you want here. Cauliflower, green beans, broccoli, corn, and anything else you want to experiment with may also work well with this recipe.

Dinner | **DAY 13**

Split Pea Soup

Makes 4 Servings

Ingredients

For the soup:

2 tablespoons NHF extra virgin olive oil

2 medium onions, finely diced

2 carrots, finely diced

2 stalks celery, finely diced

1/2 teaspoon NHF course ground black pepper

1 teaspoon NHF kosher salt

1 teaspoon NHF ground cumin

4 cloves garlic, minced

2 cups green split peas, picked over to remove rocks

3 1/4 cups vegetable stock or water

1/4 cup NHF red wine vinegar

For the garnish:

2 ripe tomatoes, diced

2 tablespoons Italian parsley, finely chopped

Method

For the lentils:

1. Heat the olive oil in a large pot. Add the onion, celery, and carrot and sauté until translucent, about 4 minutes.

2. Add the dry mustard powder, garlic, and split peas and stir to combine.

3. Add the vegetable stock, and simmer for 15-20 minutes, stirring every now and then. If it doesn't look soupy enough, add more water to thin out.

4. Swirl in the vinegar and add salt and pepper to taste.

5. May be made the night before.

For the garnish:

1. Toss together the diced tomatoes and parsley.

For the assembly:

1. Ladle the soup into four bowls to serve.

2. Sprinkle the tomatoes in a small pile in the center of the bowl.

Breakfast | DAY 14

Tofu Scramble with Potato Hash

Makes 4 Servings

Ingredients

For the scramble:

2 teaspoons NHF ground cumin

1 teaspoon NHF Herbs de Provence

1/2 teaspoon NHF ground turmeric

1 teaspoon NHF kosher salt

2 tablespoons water

1 tablespoon NHF extra virgin olive oil

1 pound extra-firm tofu, drained torn into bite size pieces

4 garlic cloves, peeled and minced

2 tablespoons nutritional yeast

1 red bell pepper, diced

For the potato hash:

2 russet potatoes, peeled and diced

1 tablespoon NHF kosher salt

1/4 cup NHF extra virgin olive oil

1 onion, diced

2 teaspoons NHF paprika

1 teaspoon NHF ground cumin

1/4 cup Italian parsley, finely chopped

Method

For the scramble:

1. Mix together the spices and water in a small cup.
2. Heat a large sauté pan with the olive oil.
3. Add the tofu and peppers, and cook for 10 minutes, letting it brown on at least one side. A thin metal spatula is necessary to make sure the tofu does not stick to the bottom of the pan.
4. Add the garlic and spices, and sauté for 1 minute more.
5. Place on the plate next to potatoes.

For the potato hash:

1. Place the potatoes in a pot and cover with 2 inches of water. Add in the salt.
2. Bring the potatoes to a boil, and boil for 10 minutes, until they are tender when pricked with a fork.
3. Drain in a colander in the sink, and plunge into a large bowl of ice water to cool down. (Alternatively, cook the night before and place in a bowl of water in the fridge for use the following day). Drain potatoes again.
4. Place the olive oil in a sauté pan and heat until simmering.
5. Add the potatoes in a single layer and let fry until golden brown. Turn over and fry the other side.
6. Add the onions and spices, and cook, stirring with the potatoes until starting to brown. Remove from heat and stir in Italian parsley.
7. Place on the plate and sprinkle with more parsley.

Lunch | **DAY 14**

Stir-Fried Tamarind Eggplant with Peppers and Thai Basil

Makes 4 Servings

Ingredients

For the fish sauce:

1/2 cup shredded seaweed, such as wakame

2 cups water

3 garlic cloves, smashed

1 teaspoon whole peppercorns

1/4 cup dried shiitake mushrooms

2 teaspoons white miso

For the tamarind sauce:

2 tablespoons soy sauce

2 tablespoons NHF apple cider vinegar

1 tablespoon tamarind paste

1/2 inch fresh ginger, finely minced or grated on a Microplane grater

2 teaspoons honey

1 teaspoon cornstarch

For the stir fry:

2 lbs Japanese eggplants, diced

1/4 cup vegetable oil

2 teaspoons NHF kosher salt

2 cloves garlic

1 red bell pepper

1 small Thai chili, seeds removed using gloved hands

1/2 cup Thai basil leaves

For the rice noodles:

1 lb rice noodles

1/2 cup peanuts, crushed and toasted

1/2 cup scallions, sliced into thin rounds

Method

For the fish sauce:

1. Combine all ingredients except the miso in a small sauce pan and simmer for 20 minutes.

2. Strain and stir in the miso. May be kept in the refrigerator up to 2 weeks.

For the tamarind sauce:

1. Place all the ingredients in a bowl and whisk to combine. Make sure there are no clumps of cornstarch or globs of honey left.

For the stir fry:

1. Add 1 tablespoon of the vegetable oil to a large heavy-bottomed pan and heat until simmering.

2. Add half the eggplant and a pinch of salt. Brown the eggplant on one side, about 2 minutes. Transfer to a bowl.

3. Stir-fry the rest of the eggplant in the same manner. Transfer to the bowl.

4. Head the last tablespoon of vegetable oil in the pan and add the garlic and peppers. Stir fry for 1 minute.

5. Add the eggplants with their juices back to the pan and pour the tamarind sauce over.

6. Stir for 1 minute more, until the sauce is glossy and coats the eggplant.

7. Transfer to a bowl and toss with the Thai basil leaves.

For the rice noodles:

1. Place the rice noodles in a very large heat-proof mixing bowl (an empty stock pot works well for this).
2. In a different pot or kettle, bring 2 quarts of water to a boil.
3. Turn the water off the heat and let cool for 2 minutes, then pour the hot water over the rice noodles to cover them. Stir with a spoon to break up the noodles.
4. Cook for 4-7 minutes, until the noodles are al dente. The bowl should not be on a heat source!
5. Drain the noodles in a colander and run under cool water to stop the cooking.

For the assembly:

1. Place the rice noodles in a bowl. Top with a large spoonful of the tamarind eggplant.
2. Top with chopped peanuts and scallions.

Dinner | **DAY 14**

Vegetable Parsley Soup

Makes 4 Servings

Ingredients

For the soup:

2 tablespoons NHF extra virgin olive oil

1/2 yellow onion, diced

1 medium carrots, peeled and sliced into rounds

2 stalks celery, diced

1/2 cup cauliflower florets, about a quarter of a head of cauliflower

1 small potato, peeled and diced

3 garlic cloves

3 teaspoons NHF Italian seasoning

2 bay leaves

1 14 oz can diced tomatoes

1 teaspoon NHF kosher salt, or to taste

1/2 teaspoon NHF black pepper, or to taste

5 cups vegetable stock

1 lemon, juiced

1/2 cup green beans, fresh or frozen sliced into 1 inch sections

1/2 cup shelled peas, fresh or frozen

1/2 cup fresh dill leaves, chopped or 3 tablespoons dried

For the garnish:

1/2 cup parsley, a few sprigs reserved for garnish

1/4 cup NHF lemon olive oil

Method

For the lentils:

1. Place a soup pot over high heat. Once the pot is hot, add extra virgin olive oil.

2. Add the onion, carrot, celery, potato, cauliflower, and Italian seasoning and cook over high heat for 4 minutes, until the onions are soft and the herbs are fragrant. If you are using dried dill, add it here.

3. Add the garlic and season with some of the salt and pepper.

4. Add tomatoes with their juices, bay leaves, lemon juice, and stock, and simmer for 15 minutes, until the potatoes and carrots are tender when pricked with a fork.

5. Add in the green beans, peas, and fresh parsley, if using. Simmer for another 5 minutes, until the green beans are tender but not browned.

6. Adjust seasoning with salt and pepper.

For the garnish:

1. Place the parsley and lemon olive oil in a blender and puree until combined.

2. Strain in a fine-mesh strainer and discard the dill solids. You should be left with a green lemon oil.

For the assembly:

1. Set out 4 soup bowls. Ladle the soup into the bowls.

2. Drizzle the oil over the top of the soup and garnish with fresh dill.

Breakfast | **DAY 15**

Cornmeal Griddle Cakes with Avocado and Tomato Jam

Makes 12 Griddle Cakes

Ingredients

For the griddle cakes:

3 teaspoons NHF extra virgin olive oil

1 tablespoon flaxseed meal

2 tablespoons water

1/4 cup applesauce

3/4 cup almond milk

1/2 cup fine ground cornmeal

1/2 cup all-purpose flour

1/2 teaspoon NHF kosher salt

2 teaspoons baking powder

2 avocados, sliced into long thin pieces

For the tomato jam:

6 roma tomatoes, finely diced

1 cup honey

2 tablespoons NHF cider vinegar

1 tablespoon ginger, finely minced or grated on a Microplane grater

1 teaspoon NHF ground cumin

1/4 teaspoon NHF ground cinnamon

1/4 teaspoon NHF ground cloves

1 teaspoon NHF kosher salt

1/2 jalapeno pepper, finely diced and half the seeds removed. Use gloves!

Method

For the griddle cakes:

1. Place the flaxseed meal in the bowl of water and let sit for 5 minutes.
2. Whisk in the applesauce, almond milk, cornmeal, and salt.
3. Fold in the flour and baking powder, taking care not to mix the batter too much.
4. Heat a 12" skillet with 1 tablespoon olive oil. Put 3 large spoonfuls of batter in the pan.
5. Cook until bubbles start to form on the top and the bottoms are light brown, about 3-5 minutes.
6. Flip over and cook until the bottom is also light brown. Place on a plate.
7. Repeat with remaining batter until it is all gone.

For the tomato jam:

1. Place all the ingredients in a small pot. Bring to a boil.
2. Simmer for 30 minutes, or until it is a jammy consistency.

For the assembly:

1. Place 4 small griddle cakes on a plate.
2. Top with a dollop of tomato jam, and lay a couple slices of avocado over the top.

Lunch | **DAY 15**

Soba Noodles with Miso-Glazed Eggplant

Makes 4 Servings

Ingredients

For the eggplant:

4 Japanese eggplants, diced

2 tablespoons NHF kosher salt

1 tablespoon NHF extra virgin olive oil

For the soba noodles:

1 lb soba noodles

For the miso vinaigrette:

1 tablespoon miso paste

1/4 cup rice wine vinegar

2 teaspoons honey

2 teaspoons Dijon mustard

1 teaspoon NHF kosher salt

1 teaspoon NHF course ground black pepper

1/3 cup NHF extra virgin olive oil

1/2 inch knob ginger, minced or grated on a Microplane grater

For the assembly:

1 bunch spring onions, greens cut into rounds

Method

For the eggplant:

1. Sprinkle the salt over the eggplants and let sit for 10 minutes in a colander in a sink. The eggplants will bead liquid.
2. Wash the salt and liquid off the eggplants.
3. Place a sauté pan over high heat and add 1 tablespoon olive oil. When it is simmering, add the eggplant and sauté until the eggplant has shrunk and is browned on one side.
4. Remove the eggplant from the pan with a slotted spoon and place in a bowl.

For the vinaigrette:

1. Place all ingredients in a bowl and whisk to combine.
2. Heat the grill or grill pan.
3. Place the eggplants cut side down on the grill and grill for 10-15 minutes, until the flesh is soft and the skin is starting to shrivel.
4. Brush the glaze onto the eggplants and place back on the grill skin side down. Cover the grill and let cook for 4 minutes, until the glaze is bubbling.

For the soba noodles:

1. Bring a large pot of water to boil. DO NOT put salt in it.
2. Submerge the soba noodles in the boiling water, using a spoon to press down to make sure they are all submerged.
3. Cook for 5-8 minutes, or according to the package instructions. The noodles should be cooked through, not chewy "al dente", but also not mushy.
4. Drain the noodles into a colander and vigorously use your hands to rub the noodles under the running water to get all the starch off of them.
5. Place into a bowl.

For the assembly:

1. Toss the soba noodles with the eggplant and half the vinaigrette. Taste for salt and pepper and strength of vinaigrette. Add more salt and vinaigrette if you think it needs it.
2. Place dressed noodles into a bowl and garnish with scallions.

Dinner | **DAY 15**

Sweet Pea Soup with Mint and Cashew Cream

Makes 4 Servings

Ingredients

For the soup:

2 tablespoons NHF extra virgin olive oil

1 onion, diced

1 fennel bulb, medium dice

1/4 cup mint leaves, chopped

1/4 cup Italian parsley leaves, chopped

6 cups shelled peas, fresh or frozen

4 cups vegetable stock

1 teaspoon NHF kosher salt, or to taste

1/2 teaspoon NHF ground white pepper, or to taste

For the cashew cream:

1/2 cup raw cashews, preferably soaked for 2-3 hours

1/4 cup water, + 1-2 tablespoons as needed for thinning

1 tablespoon NHF apple cider vinegar

1 teaspoon NHF kosher salt

Chives, chopped into fine rounds

Method

For the soup:

1. Place a soup pot over high heat. Once the pot is hot, add extra virgin olive oil.

2. Add the onion and fennel and cook over high heat for 4 minutes, stirring constantly, until they start to soften.

3. Add the carrot and garlic and season with some of the salt and pepper.

4. Add the peas and stock, and simmer for 5 minutes, or until the peas turn bright green but not brown. Turn the heat off.

5. Add the mint and Italian parsley.

6. Using a drink blender, puree the mixture until it is completely smooth. Check that it is thick enough to coat the back of a spoon. You may need to add a bit more stock or water to thin the mixture out.

7. Add salt and pepper to taste. Do not boil the soup or it will turn brown.

For the cashew cream:

1. Place all the ingredients except the chives in a small food processor. Blend until smooth.

For the assembly:

1. Set out 4 soup bowls. Ladle the soup into the bowls.

2. Drizzle the cream around the soup and top with chopped chives.

Breakfast | **DAY 16**

Mixed Potatoes Breakfast Tacos

Makes 4 Servings

Ingredients

For the potatoes:

1 medium sweet potato, peeled and diced

1 Idaho potato, peeled and diced

1 red pepper, diced

1 yellow pepper, diced

1/4 cup NHF olive oil

2 teaspoons NHF kosher salt

1 teaspoon NHF ground black pepper

For the black beans:

1/2 pound black beans, rinsed and picked over

1 medium yellow onion, peeled and quartered

4 cloves garlic, mashed

3 bay leaves

1 teaspoon ground cloves

1 gallon water

2 tablespoons NHF kosher salt

1 tablespoon NHF red wine vinegar

For the pico de gallo:

1 red onion, finely diced

3 roma tomatoes, finely diced

1/4 cup cilantro leaves, finely chopped, plus more for garnish

1 lime, juiced

1 teaspoon NHF kosher salt

For the assembly:

2 tablespoons cilantro, chopped

3 cilantro leaves

1 lemon sliced into 8 wedges

8 corn tortillas

Method

For the mixed potatoes:

1. Preheat the oven to 375°F.
2. Place the diced potatoes on a sheet pan and drizzle with olive oil and a pinch of salt.
3. Roast in the oven until starting to brown and tender when pierced with a fork, about 10 minutes.

For the black beans:

1. Place the beans in a colander in the sink and rinse to get rid of any dirt. Pick out any rocks or twigs that you might see as well.
2. Transfer the beans to a large pot and cover with four inches of cold water. Let soak overnight or up to 24 hours.
3. Drain and rinse the beans in a colander, and return to the pot. Add the onion, garlic, bay leaves, cloves, and water.
4. Place over medium-high heat until the water comes to a boil. Reduce the heat to medium-low to keep it at a simmer.
5. Simmer for 30-40 minutes, or until the beans are soft but not falling apart. Remove from heat and stir in salt and red wine vinegar. Mash with a potato masher.

For the pico de gallo:

1. Place all the ingredients in a bowl and mix well; adjust seasoning with NHF salt and pepper.

For the assembly:

1. Place the corn tortillas over an open flame one at a time and warm them slightly (you can also place them into a preheated oven).
2. On each warm tortilla, place a spoonful of black bean paste and smear around.
3. Place 2 spoonfuls of the mixed potatoes on top.
4. Place 1 spoonful of pico de gallo atop the potatoes.
5. Place the 2 tacos on each serving plate, sprinkle with chopped cilantro, cilantro leaf and 2 lime wedges.

Lunch | **DAY 16**

Penne Arrabiata

Makes 4 Servings

Ingredients

For the penne:

1 lb quinoa penne noodles

2 tablespoons NHF extra virgin olive oil

1 tablespoon NHF kosher salt

For the Arrabiata sauce:

2 tablespoons NHF extra virgin olive oil

2 cups cherry tomatoes, sliced in half

1 tablespoon red pepper flakes

2 tablespoons tomato paste

1 tablespoon plus more to taste NHF kosher salt

1/2 teaspoon NHF course black pepper

2 tablespoons basil, sliced into a thin chiffonade

For the garnish:

1/4 cup basil, sliced into thin strips

1/4 cup Italian parsley, finely chopped

Method

For the pasta:

1. Bring a large pot of water to boil. Add a tablespoon of salt to the water.
2. Cook the spaghetti according to package instructions, usually 7-8 minutes at a rolling boil.
3. When it is done cooking, drain it in a colander. Reserve 1 cup of the cooking liquid.
4. Place back in the pot and toss with 2 tablespoons of olive oil, or enough to coat it so that it does not stick together.

For the sauce:

1. Heat a large sauté pan on the stove; add 2 tablespoons olive oil.
2. Add the tomato paste and red pepper flakes, and stir until fragrant.
3. Add the tomatoes and remove from heat.
4. Stir in the pasta and 1/4 cup of the cooking liquid. If it looks too dry and is sticking to the pan, add 1/4 cup more of the liquid at a time.

For the assembly:

1. Place the pasta in a pasta bowl.
2. Sprinkle the sliced basil and chopped parsley over the top of the pasta.

Hints:

- To chiffonade basil, stack 5 leaves of basil on top of each other and roll into a cigar shape. Thinly slice the roll and unfurl to create thin strips.

Dinner | **DAY 16**

Sweet Potato Soup with Fried Sage

Makes 4 Servings

Ingredients

For the soup:

16 oz sweet potato, peeled and diced large

2 large parsnip, peeled and diced large

1/2 Spanish onion, peeled and diced large

2 celery stalks, diced large

1 large carrot, peeled and diced large

NHF Kosher salt, as needed

NHF ground black pepper, as needed

NHF extra virgin olive oil, as needed

4 garlic cloves

1/2 cup white wine

4 cups vegetable broth

Water, as needed

For the sage:

1/4 cup vegetable oil

Kosher salt, as needed

1/4 cup sage leaves, packed

2 teaspoons NHF lemon olive oil

Method

For the soup:

1. Place a soup pot over high heat. Once the pot is hot, add extra virgin olive oil.
2. Add the sweet potatoes, parsnip, onions, carrots, and celery. Stir well and cook over high heat for 4 minutes.
3. Add the garlic and red pepper flakes and season with some salt and pepper.
4. Add the wine and bring to a boil.
5. Add enough vegetable stock to cover the vegetables, bring back to a boil, and cook for 25 minutes or until fork tender over medium heat.
6. Remove from heat.
7. Using a drink or a stick blender, mix the chunky soup into a smooth-textured soup.
8. Please blend the soup carefully. You will need to let each batch run for about 2-3 minutes to reach the desired smooth consistency. Remove from the blender into a clean pot.
9. Once you blend all the soup, place the pot on low heat. Adjust seasoning with salt and pepper and the thickness by adding water if needed. Please note that the consistency should be such that the soup will stick to the spoon.
10. Do not boil the soup—simply bring it to a hot temperature and serve immediately.

For the sage:

1. Place the olive oil in a small pan and heat until simmering.
2. Add the whole sage leaves and cook until crispy.
3. Remove from oil with a slotted spoon and place on a plate lined with paper towels. Sprinkle lightly with salt.

For the assembly:

1. Place the soup in a bowl, and place the fried sage in the center of the soup.
2. Drizzle some lemon oil around the sage.

Breakfast | **DAY 17**

Hummus, Tomato, and Arugula Toast

Makes 4 Servings

Ingredients

For the hummus:

1 can chickpeas, drained approx 1 cup

2 tablespoons water

1 clove garlic

2 teaspoons NHF kosher salt, or to taste

1/4 cup tahini paste

Juice from 1 lemon

1 teaspoon NHF ground cumin

1/2 teaspoon NHF paprika

2 tablespoons NHF extra virgin olive oil

For the toast:

8 slices whole wheat bread, toasted

1 cup hummus

2 roma tomatoes, finely diced

2 cups fresh arugula, rinsed and dried

1 teaspoon NHF kosher salt

4 scallions, finely sliced

Method

For the hummus:

1. Put the chickpeas, garlic, salt, cumin, paprika, tahini, and water in a blender and turn on low. With the blender running, slowly drizzle in the olive oil.

2. Blend until smooth, adding more olive oil as needed to thin out the hummus and create a completely smooth texture. Taste for salt and add more if needed.

3. May be made in advance. Will keep in the refrigerator for up to one week.

For the assembly:

1. Spread a thin layer of hummus on each slice of toast.

2. Top with diced tomatoes and sprinkle a pinch of salt on top.

3. Garnish with a handful of sliced scallions followed by a handful of arugula.

Hints:

- Using store-bought hummus is a great time-saver!
- Slicing scallions diagonally creates a beautiful, restaurant-quality presentation.

Lunch | **DAY 17**

Fettuccini With Mushroom Cream Sauce

Makes 4 Servings

Ingredients

For the pasta:

1 lb quinoa fettuccini pasta
2 tablespoons NHF extra virgin olive oil
1 tablespoon NHF kosher salt

For the mushrooms:

2 tablespoons NHF extra virgin olive oil
1 lb mushrooms, oyster or shiitake
1/2 medium yellow onion
4 cloves garlic, minced
3 tablespoons fresh thyme, finely chopped
1/2 teaspoon NHF ground cinnamon
2 tablespoons NHF Italian seasoning
1/2 cup white wine
1 teaspoon NHF kosher salt, or to taste
1/2 teaspoon NHF course black pepper
1 14 oz can coconut milk
1/2 cup vegetable stock
1/4 cup cornstarch
2 tablespoons water

For the garnish:

1/4 cup Italian parsley, finely chopped but hold back a few whole leaves
NHF course ground black pepper

Method

For the pasta:

1. Bring a large pot of water to boil. Add a tablespoon of salt to the water.
2. Cook the fettuccini according to package instructions, usually 7-8 minutes at a rolling boil.
3. When it is done cooking, drain it in a colander. Reserve 1 cup of the cooking liquid.
4. Place back in the pot and toss with 2 tablespoons of olive oil, or enough to coat it so that it does not stick together.

For the mushrooms:

1. Brush dirt off mushrooms using a pastry brush. Slice into 1/4 inch long slivers.
2. Put 1 tablespoon oil in a large sauté pan. Once it is simmering, place the mushrooms in a single layer.
3. Let the mushrooms brown, 3-4 minutes, then turn over or stir to brown the other side. Pour into a bowl. Repeat with remaining mushrooms, working in small batches.
4. Once all the mushrooms are done, deglaze the pan with the white wine, scraping the bottom of the pan with a wooden spoon to get all the browned bits incorporated.
5. Add the onions, Italian seasoning, and cinnamon and cook until softened.
6. Add the garlic and thyme and cook 1 minute more.
7. Pour the coconut milk and vegetable stock into the cooking onions and add the mushrooms back in. Add salt and pepper to taste.
8. In a small bowl, combine the cornstarch and water. Whisk until no clumps of cornstarch remain.
9. Add cornstarch into the pasta sauce; cook until the liquids have reduced by half and the sauce coats the back of a spoon.
10. Stir in the pasta and cook to coat.

For the assembly:

1. Place the pasta in a pasta bowl and twirl with tongs to make a pretty vortex. Make sure there are some mushrooms visible on top of the middle of the pasta.

2. Sprinkle Italian parsley on the center of the bowl, making sure not to cover up all the mushrooms. Add a single whole leaf of parsley to the very center.

3. Sprinkle with cracked black pepper. A pepper grinder works great for this.

Dinner | **DAY 17**

Carrot Ginger Soup

Makes 4 Servings

Ingredients

For the soup:

5 large carrots, peeled and diced

1 parsnip, peeled and diced large

1 Spanish onion, peeled and diced large

2 celery stalks, diced large

NHF Kosher salt, as needed

NHF course ground black pepper, as needed

NHF extra virgin olive oil, as needed

4 garlic cloves

2 inch knob of ginger, peeled and grated on a Microplane grater

1/2 cup coconut milk

4 cups vegetable broth

Water, as needed

For the garnish:

2 tablespoons sesame seeds, toasted

NHF olive oil, for drizzling

Method

For the soup:

1. Place a soup pot over high heat. Once the pot is hot, add extra virgin olive oil.
2. Add the carrots, parsnip, onions, and celery. Stir well and cook over high heat for 4 minutes.
3. Add the garlic and ginger and season with some salt and pepper.
4. Add enough vegetable stock to cover the vegetables, bring back to a boil and cook for 25 minutes or until fork tender over medium heat.
5. Stir in the coconut milk.
6. Remove from heat using a drink blender; mix the chunky soup into a smooth textured soup.
7. Please blend the soup carefully. You will need to let each batch run for about 2-3 minutes to reach the desired smooth consistency. Remove from the blender into a clean pot.
8. Once you blend all the soup, place the pot on low heat. Adjust seasoning with salt and pepper and the thickness by adding water if needed. Please note that the consistency should be such that the soup will stick to the spoon.
9. Do not boil the soup—simply bring it to a hot temperature and serve immediately.

For the assembly:

1. Place the soup in a bowl, and place the sesame seeds in the center of the soup.
2. Drizzle some olive oil around the bowl.

Breakfast | **DAY 18**

Chimichurri Breakfast Burrito

Makes 4 Servings

Ingredients

For the chimichurri:

4 garlic cloves

1 cup cilantro leaves, loosely packed

1/2 cup Italian parsley leaves, loosely packed

2 tablespoons fresh oregano, leaves stripped from stems

1/4 cup NHF red wine vinegar

1/4 cup NHF extra virgin olive oil

NHF kosher salt, to taste

NHF course ground black pepper, to taste

1 shallot

For the potato hash:

3 russet potatoes, peeled and diced

1 tablespoon NHF kosher salt

1 tablespoon soy sauce or tamari

1/4 cup NHF extra virgin olive oil

1 onion, diced

1 red bell pepper, diced

4 large whole wheat tortillas

Method

For the chimichurri:

1. Place cilantro, parsley, and shallot in a food processor and chop.
2. Add remaining ingredients, and process until smooth. Add salt and pepper to taste.

For the potato hash:

1. Place the potatoes in a pot and cover with 2 inches of water. Add in the salt.
2. Bring the potatoes to a boil and boil for 10 minutes, until they are tender when pricked with a fork.
3. Drain in a colander in the sink, and plunge into a large bowl of ice water to cool down. (Alternatively, cook the night before and place in a bowl of water in the fridge for use the following day). Drain potatoes again.
4. Toss potatoes in soy sauce.
5. Place the olive oil in a sauté pan and heat until simmering.
6. Add the potatoes (but not the soy sauce!) in a single layer and let fry until golden brown. Turn over and fry the other side.
7. Add the onions, bell peppers, and spices, and cook, stirring with the potatoes, until starting to brown. Remove from heat.

For the assembly:

1. Lay out 4 whole wheat tortillas and evenly divide the potatoes, placing in the middle.
2. Spoon chimichurri sauce over the potatoes
3. Roll up the tortilla.

Lunch | **DAY 18**

Grilled Portabello Sandwiches

Makes 4 Servings

Ingredients

For the marinade and mushrooms:

3 roma tomatoes, pureed in a blender

Juice from 1 orange, about 1/2 cup

Juice from 2 lemons, about 1/2 cup

1/4 cup soy sauce or tamari

1/3 cup honey

2 teaspoons NHF ground cumin

1/2 teaspoon NHF ground cinnamon

1 teaspoon NHF kosher salt

2 teaspoons minced fresh ginger

1 tablespoon NHF balsamic vinegar

4 large portabello mushrooms

For the chipotle mayo:

1 cup vegan mayonnaise

1 tablespoon chipotle peppers in adobo sauce, SAUCE ONLY (comes in a can, usually in the Mexican aisle of the supermarket)

For the sandwiches:

4 whole wheat buns

1 cup chipotle mayo

16 tomato slices, 2 per sandwich

16 slices of pickles, 4 per sandwich

1/2 red onion, thinly sliced

Method

For the marinade:

1. Place all the ingredients in a jar and shake to combine.
2. Place the mushrooms in a shallow baking pan, sprinkle salt over, and cover with marinade. Let sit for a minimum of 15 minutes, up to overnight.

For the grilled mushrooms:

1. Heat the grill or grill pan.
2. Place mushrooms on the grill, and grill until dark grill marks are visible, approx. 3-4 minutes.
3. Turnover and grill another 3-4 minutes.
4. Transfer to a clean platter. Repeat with remaining mushrooms.

For the chipotle mayo:

1. Place all the ingredients into a bowl, mix well.
2. Place aside.

For the assembly:

1. Lay out 2 slices of bread.
2. Spread about 1 tablespoon of chipotle mayo on each bun.
3. Slice mushrooms on the diagonal and fan out over a slice of bun.
4. Place 2 slices of tomatoes and 4 slices of pickles on top of the tomatoes, and place the sliced onions atop of the pickles. Cover with other slice of bread.

Hints:

- Chipotle in adobo sauce can be substitute for chipotle hot sauce such as tabasco or Cholula brands.

Dinner | **DAY 18**

Chunky Vegetable Soup

Makes 4 Servings

Ingredients

For the soup:

2 tablespoons NHF extra virgin olive oil

1 yellow onion, diced

2 medium yellow carrots, peeled and diced

2 stalks celery, diced

1 medium potato, peeled and diced

1 cup corn, fresh or frozen

2 garlic cloves

1 tablespoon NHF Italian seasoning

1 teaspoon NHF kosher salt, or to taste

1/2 teaspoon NHF course ground black pepper, or to taste

1 can diced tomatoes

3 cups vegetable stock

3/4 cup green beans, sliced in half

1/2 cup frozen spinach

For the garnish:

1 small bunch Italian parsley, finely chopped

Method

For the soup:

1. Place a soup pot over high heat. Once the pot is hot, add extra virgin olive oil.
2. Add the onion, carrot, celery, potato, Italian seasoning, red pepper flakes, and bay leaf and cook over high heat for 4 minutes, until the onions are soft.
3. Add the garlic and season with some of the salt and pepper.
4. Add tomatoes with their juices, corn, stock, and simmer for 15 minutes.
5. Add in the frozen spinach and green beans and cook just until heated through and bright green.
6. Add salt and pepper to taste.

For the assembly:

1. Set out 4 soup bowls. Ladle the soup into the bowls.
2. Sprinkle Italian parsley over the center of the soup.

Breakfast | **DAY 19**

Roasted Red Pepper Hummus with Toast

Makes 4 Servings

Ingredients

For the hummus:

1 can chickpeas, drained approx 1 cup

2 tablespoons water

1 clove garlic

2 teaspoons NHF kosher salt, or to taste

1/4 cup tahini paste

Juice from 1 lemon

1 teaspoon NHF ground cumin

1/2 teaspoon NHF paprika

2 tablespoons NHF extra virgin olive oil

1 roasted red pepper, thinly sliced, reserve 1/4 of it for garnish

For the red peppers:

1 red pepper

For the assembly:

4 slices whole wheat toast

1/4 roasted red pepper, finely diced

2 teaspoons NHF lemon extra virgin olive oil

Method

For the hummus:

1. Put the chickpeas, garlic, salt, cumin, paprika, tahini, roasted red pepper, and water in a blender and turn on low. With the blender running, slowly drizzle in the olive oil.

2. Blend until smooth, adding more olive oil as needed to thin out the hummus and create a completely smooth texture. Taste for salt and add more if needed.

3. May be made in advance. Will keep in the refrigerator for up to one week.

For the pepper:

1. Place the pepper directly on the flame of a burner turned to high heat.

2. Once one side is fully blackened, use metal tongs to turn slightly. Keep rotating the pepper until all sides are fully blackened.

3. Once it is fully blackened, place in a large bowl and cover with plastic wrap. Let it sit for 5 minutes to loosen the skin.

4. Gently rub the blackened skin off the red pepper.

5. Slice into thin slices. May be kept in the fridge for up to 3 days.

For the assembly:

1. Spread a thin layer of hummus on each slice of toast, making a slight indent in the center.

2. Place the diced red peppers into the indent and drizzle olive oil on the top of the toast.

Hints:

- You may use store-bought hummus and blend with the red pepper to make the red pepper hummus.

- The pepper may be roasted the night before and kept in the refrigerator.

Lunch | **DAY 19**

Polenta Casserole with Mushrooms and Swiss Chard

Makes 4 Servings

Ingredients

For the polenta:

2 cups water

2 cups vegetable stock

2 cups uncooked polenta

1 teaspoon NHF kosher salt

For the mushrooms:

2 tablespoons NHF extra virgin olive oil

1 lb mushrooms, oyster or cremini, cleaned and sliced

1/2 medium yellow onion

4 cloves garlic, minced

3 tablespoons fresh thyme, finely chopped

2 tablespoons NHF Italian seasoning

1/2 cup white wine

1 teaspoon NHF kosher salt, or to taste

1/2 teaspoon NHF course ground black pepper

1 bunch Swiss chard, stems removed and leaves sliced

Method

For the polenta:

1. Oil an 8x8 baking dish.
2. Bring the water and vegetable stock to a boil on the stove.
3. Add the polenta and stock, and stir constantly to mix thoroughly, about 15 minutes. It will expand and thicken.
4. Once all the water is absorbed, pour into prepared baking dish.

For the mushrooms:

1. Brush dirt off mushrooms using a pastry brush. Slice into 1/4 inch long slivers.
2. Put 1 tablespoon oil in a large sauté pan. Once it is simmering, place the mushrooms in a single layer.
3. Let the mushrooms brown, 3-4 minutes, then turn over or stir to brown the other side. Pour into a bowl. Repeat with remaining mushrooms, working in small batches.
4. Once all the mushrooms are done, deglaze the pan with the white wine, scraping the bottom of the pan with a wooden spoon to get all the browned bits incorporated.
5. Add the onions, Italian seasoning, and Swiss chard and cook until softened. You might need a bit more olive oil.
6. Add the garlic and thyme and cook 1 minute more.
7. Pour on top of the polenta and gently press into the top.

For the assembly:

1. Bake the polenta with mushrooms and chard topping for 10 minutes to bind the flavors.
2. Slice into 4x4 squares to serve; may be eaten cold.

Dinner | DAY 19

Mexican Tortilla Soup

Makes 4 Servings

Ingredients

For the soup:

1/4 cup NHF extra virgin olive oil

1/2 yellow onion, diced

4 garlic cloves

1 tablespoon tomato paste

1 tablespoon NHF chili powder

1 teaspoon NHF ground cumin

1 teaspoon NHF kosher salt, or to taste

1/2 teaspoon NHF course ground black pepper, or to taste

1 can diced tomatoes

1 can black beans, rinsed and drained

3 cups vegetable stock

1/2 cup cilantro leaves, finely chopped

For the tortilla strips:

4 corn tortillas, cut into strips 2 inches long by 1/4 inch

1/4 cup vegetable oil

1 teaspoon NHF kosher salt, or to taste

1 small bunch cilantro leaves, finely chopped

For the cashew cream:

1/2 cup raw cashews, preferably soaked for 2-3 hours

1/4 cup water, + 1-2 tablespoons as needed for thinning

1/2 lime, juiced

1/2 teaspoon NHF kosher salt

Method

For the soup:

1. Place a soup pot over high heat. Once the pot is hot, add extra virgin olive oil.
2. Add the onion and cook over high heat for 4 minutes, until it is soft.
3. Add the garlic, tomato paste, chili powder, and cumin, and season with some of the salt and pepper.
4. Add tomatoes with their juices, beans, and stock, and simmer for 15 minutes.
5. Stir in the cilantro leaves and add salt and pepper to taste.

For the tortilla strips:

1. Heat the oil in a sauté pan until simmering.
2. Add the tortilla strips in a single layer. You will have to work in batches.
3. Fry until golden brown on one side, then using tongs or a slotted spoon, flip over and brown on the other side.
4. Using a slotted spoon, remove from the heat and place on a paper towel-lined plate to drain. Sprinkle salt over.

For the cashew cream:

1. Place all the ingredients in a small food processor. Blend until smooth.

For the assembly:

1. Set out 4 soup bowls. Ladle the soup into the bowls.
2. Place a large handful of tortilla strips in the center of the bowl and garnish with cilantro leaves and cashew cream.

Breakfast | **DAY 20**

Sweet Potato Rancheros

Makes 4 Servings

Ingredients

For the sweet potatoes:

3 large sweet potatoes, peeled and diced
2 teaspoons NHF extra virgin olive oil
2 teaspoons NHF Herbes de Provence
1 teaspoon NHF kosher salt

For the black beans:

1 pound black beans, rinsed and picked over
1 medium yellow onion, peeled and quartered
4 cloves garlic, smashed
3 bay leaves
1 teaspoon ground cloves
1 gallon water
2 tablespoons NHF kosher salt
1 tablespoon NHF red wine vinegar

For the pico de gallo:

1 red onion, finely diced
3 Roma tomatoes, finely diced
1/4 cup cilantro leaves, finely chopped, plus more for garnish
1 lime, juiced

For the tortillas:

8 corn tortillas
1 teaspoon NHF kosher salt
1/4 cup vegetable oil

For the cashew cream:

1/2 cup raw cashews, preferably soaked for 2-3 hours
1/4 cup water, + 1-2 tablespoons as needed for thinning
1 tablespoon NHF apple cider vinegar
1 teaspoon NHF kosher salt

Method

For the sweet potatoes:

1. Preheat the oven to 375°F.
2. Place the sliced sweet potatoes on a sheet pan and drizzle with olive oil and a pinch of salt.
3. Roast in the oven until starting to brown and tender when pierced with a fork, about 10 minutes.

For the black beans:

1. Place the beans in a colander in the sink and rinse to get rid of any dirt. Pick out any rocks or twigs that you might see as well.
2. Transfer the beans to a large pot and cover with four inches of cold water. Let soak overnight or up to 24 hours.
3. Drain and rinse the beans in a colander, and return to the pot. Add the onion, garlic, bay leaves, cloves, and water.
4. Place over medium-high heat until the water comes to a boil. Reduce the heat to medium-low to keep it at a simmer.
5. Simmer for 30-40 minutes, or until the beans are soft but not falling apart. Remove from heat and stir in salt and red wine vinegar. Mash with a potato masher.

For the tortillas:

1. Heat the oil in a sauté pan until simmering.
2. Add one tortilla at a time. Fry until golden brown on one side.
3. Using tongs, flip over and brown on the other side.
4. Remove from the heat and place on a paper towel-lined plate to drain. Sprinkle salt over. Repeat with remaining tortillas.

For the cashew cream:

1. Place all the ingredients in a small food processor. Blend until smooth.

For the assembly:

1. Lay out 2 corn tortillas per plate and spread mashed beans over it.
2. Top with sweet potatoes—it is okay if they overflow the tortilla.
3. Put a spoonful of pico de gallo and a dollop of cashew cream on top.
4. Garnish with chopped cilantro.

Hints:

- You may use canned black beans if you are pressed for time.

Lunch | **DAY 20**

Corn, Pepper, Black Bean, and Quinoa Burrito

Makes 4 Servings

Ingredients

For the cilantro lime dressing:

2 limes, juiced

1/4 cup cilantro leaves, finely chopped

1 teaspoon honey

1/4 cup NHF extra virgin olive oil

For the black beans:

1 pound black beans, rinsed and picked over

1 medium yellow onion, peeled and quartered

4 cloves garlic, smashed

3 bay leaves

1 teaspoon NHF ground cloves

1 gallon water

2 tablespoons NHF kosher salt

1 tablespoon NHF red wine vinegar

For the roasted red pepper:

2 red peppers

For the quinoa:

1 cup quinoa

2 cups water

1 teaspoon NHF kosher salt

2 teaspoons NHF extra virgin olive oil

1 cup corn, fresh cut off the cob or frozen

Method

For the cilantro lime dressing:

1. Mix together the lime juice and honey, stirring until the honey is dissolved.
2. Add the cilantro leaves, and slowly stream in the olive oil, whisking constantly.

For the black beans:

1. Place the beans in a colander in the sink and rinse to get rid of any dirt. Pick out any rocks or twigs that you might see as well.
2. Transfer the beans to a large pot and cover with four inches of cold water. Let soak overnight or up to 24 hours.
3. Drain and rinse the beans in a colander, and return to the pot. Add the onion, garlic, bay leaves, cloves, and water.
4. Place over medium-high heat until the water comes to a boil. Reduce the heat to medium-low to keep it at a simmer.
5. Simmer for 30-40 minutes, or until the beans are soft but not falling apart. Remove from heat and stir in salt and red wine vinegar. Cool completely, then portion into 2 cup pint containers. Containers may be frozen for up to a month.

For the pepper:

1. Place the pepper directly on the flame of a burner turned to high heat.
2. Once one side is fully blackened, use metal tongs to turn slightly. Keep rotating the pepper until all sides are fully blackened.
3. Once it is fully blackened, place in a large bowl and cover with plastic wrap. Let it sit for 5 minutes to loosen the skin.
4. Gently rub the blackened skin off the red pepper.
5. Dice the roasted pepper. May be kept in the fridge for up to 3 days.

For the quinoa:

1. Heat the olive oil in a large pot until simmering. Add the quinoa and stir until toasted and fragrant, about 2 minutes.
2. Add the salt and water and bring to a boil. Cover the pot and turn the heat down to low. Simmer for 15 minutes.
3. Remove from heat and let sit for 5 minutes. Fluff with a fork.

For the assembly:

1. Lay out 4 whole wheat tortillas and evenly divide the black beans, corn, peppers, and quinoa placing in stripes along the middle of the tortilla.
2. Spoon vinaigrette on top.
3. Roll up the tortilla.

Hints:

- You may use one 14 oz can of black beans instead of cooking your own.
- Pepper may be roasted the night before, or up to 3 days in advance. Juices will leak out as it sits—this is normal. Just drain them before using.

Dinner | **DAY 20**

Tomato, Root Vegetable, and Rice Soup

Makes 4 Servings

Ingredients

For the soup:

2 tablespoons NHF extra virgin olive oil

1 yellow onion, diced

6 garlic cloves

1 parsnip, medium diced

1 rutabaga, medium diced

2 medium turnips, medium diced

1 carrot, medium diced

1 cup cremini or white mushrooms, cleaned and sliced

1 tablespoon Italian seasoning

1 14 oz can diced tomatoes, or 5 tomatoes, diced

1/2 cup dry white wine

1/2 cup brown rice

4 cups vegetable stock

2 tablespoons NHF balsamic vinegar

1 teaspoon NHF kosher salt, or to taste

1/2 teaspoon NHF ground white pepper, or to taste

For the garnish:

1 large beet, peeled

3 tablespoons vegetable oil

NHF kosher salt

1 tablespoon Italian parsley leaves

1 tablespoon NHF lemon infused olive oil

Method

For the soup:

1. Place a soup pot over high heat. Once the pot is hot, add extra virgin olive oil.
2. Add the onion, cook over high heat for 4 minutes.
3. Add the garlic, Italian seasoning, rice, and vegetables and season with some of the salt and pepper.
4. Add the wine and cook until it evaporates.
5. Add the tomatoes, stock, and balsamic and simmer for 35-40 minutes, or until the rice is cooked. Add more stock if the soup becomes too thick.
6. Add salt and pepper to taste.

For the garnish:

1. Slice the beet thinly on a mandoline, or use a vegetable peeler to make long strips.
2. Heat olive oil in a small shallow pan until it is simmering.
3. Place the beet strips into the olive oil and fry until barely starting to brown.
4. Using a slotted spoon or tongs, remove strips from the oil and place on a paper towel to dry. Sprinkle with salt.
5. Place the lemon olive oil and parsley in a small food processor and blend until smooth. Use a fine mesh strainer to strain out the parsley leaves. You should have a green parsley oil.

For the assembly:

1. Set out 4 soup bowls. Ladle the soup into the bowls.
2. Top with beet chips and drizzle parsley oil around the soup.

Breakfast | **DAY 21**

Banana French Toast With Apple Compote

Makes 4 Servings

Ingredients

For the batter:
- 1 tablespoon flaxseeds
- 2 very ripe bananas
- 2 cups soy milk
- 1/2 teaspoon NHF nutmeg
- 1 teaspoon NHF ground cinnamon
- 1/4 teaspoon NHF kosher salt

For the French toast:
- 8 slices of whole wheat bread, left out overnight to get stale
- 1/4 cup NHF extra virgin olive oil

For the apple compote:
- 3 apples, peeled, cored, and finely diced
- 2 tablespoons maple syrup
- 1 vanilla bean, sliced length wise and scraped
- 1 cup apple juice or water
- 1/2 orange, juiced and zested
- 1 lemon, juiced
- 1/4 teaspoon NHF ground cloves
- 1/2 teaspoon NHF ground allspice
- 1/2 teaspoon NHF ground cinnamon
- 1/4 teaspoon NHF kosher salt

For the maple vegan sour cream (optional):
- 1/2 cup raw cashews
- 3 tablespoons raw slivered almonds (must be peeled)
- 1/4 cup lemon juice (from approximately 2 small lemons)
- 1/2 cup water
- 1 tablespoon NHF apple cider vinegar
- 1 tablespoon nutritional yeast
- 1 teaspoon NHF kosher salt
- 1 tablespoon maple syrup

Method

For the batter:
1. Place all the ingredients in a blender and puree until smooth.

For the French toast:
1. Preheat oven to 200°F.
2. Heat the olive oil in a sauté pan over medium heat.
3. Place the batter in a shallow bowl. Dip 2 slices of bread in the batter at a time, covering both sides, but do not let sit and get soggy. Immediately place in the hot pan.
4. Brown the bread on one side, flip over and brown the other.
5. Remove the slice from the pan with a spatula and place on a sheet tray lined with parchment paper. Place in 200 degree oven to keep warm.
6. Repeat with remaining slices of bread, adding to the same sheet tray in the oven when done.

For the apple compote:
1. In a large saucepan, combine all the ingredients and bring to a boil.
2. Reduce the heat to low and simmer until the liquid has almost evaporated, about 10 minutes.
3. Serve warm. Store in the refrigerator in an airtight container up to 4 days.

For the sour cream:
1. Soak the cashews and almonds overnight, or a minimum of 2-3 hours.
2. Drain and rinse well and put in a blender.
3. Add in the rest of the ingredients and blend until smooth. You may need to stop the blender once or twice and use a spatula to scrape down the sides to incorporate all the ingredients.
4. May be stored in the fridge for up to 10 days.

For the assembly:
1. Place 2 slices of toast overlapping on each plate.
2. Top with a large spoonful of apple compote.
3. Place a dollop of sour cream on the side (optional).

Lunch | **DAY 21**

Falafel Sandwich with Hummus, Tomatoes, Cucumber, and Red Onion

Makes 4 Servings

Ingredients

For the falafel:

- **1** 15 oz can chickpeas
- **2** tablespoons Italian parsley, finely chopped
- **2** tablespoons cilantro, finely chopped
- **4** green onions, finely diced
- **3** large garlic cloves, roughly chopped
- **1 1/2** teaspoons NHF cumin
- **1** lemon, juiced and zested
- **1** teaspoon NHF kosher salt
- **1 1/2** teaspoons baking powder
- **1/3** cup flour, plus more for shaping patties
- **1** cup vegetable oil

For the hummus:

- **1** can chickpeas, drained approx 1 cup
- **2** tablespoons water
- **1** clove garlic
- **2** teaspoons NHF kosher salt, or to taste
- **1/4** cup plus 2 tablespoons tahini paste
- Juice from 1 lemon
- **1** teaspoon NHF ground cumin
- **1/2** teaspoon NHF paprika
- **2** tablespoons NHF extra virgin olive oil

For the sandwiches:

- **8** slices whole wheat bread, toasted
- **16** slices Roma tomatoes, from about 5
- **16** slices cucumber
- **1** red onion, sliced into thin slivers

Method

For the falafel:

1. Place the chickpeas, onions, spices, and herbs in the bowl of a food processor.
2. Process until all the large chunks are gone, but it does not need to be smooth. Stop the processor and scrape down the sides of the bowl a couple of times to get all the large clumps off the sides.
3. Add in the baking powder and pulse to combine.
4. Transfer to a bowl and add flour 1 tablespoon at a time, mixing until it is completely combined. Once the mixture is firm enough to form into a ball, you have added enough flour; it will take 4-5 tablespoons total.
5. Place in the refrigerator to chill for 20 minutes.
6. Add enough oil to a sauté pan to come 1/2 inch up the sides. Place a plate lined with paper towels next to the stove.
7. Take 2 tablespoons of chickpea mixture out of the food processor and, with hands covered in flour, roll into a ball.
8. Once the oil is simmering, add the ball to the pan. You may put as many falafels in the pan as can fit with enough room to turn around.
9. Once they are browned on one side, turn over using metal tongs to brown evenly all over. Once browned, remove from the oil and place on the towel-lined plate.

For the hummus:

1. Put the chickpeas, garlic, salt, cumin, paprika, tahini, and water in a blender and turn on low. With the blender running, slowly drizzle in the olive oil.
2. Blend until smooth, adding more olive oil as needed to thin out the hummus and create a completely smooth texture. Taste for salt and add more if needed.
3. May be made in advance. Will keep in the refrigerator up to one week.

For the assembly:

1. Lay out 2 slices of bread.
2. Spread a thin layer of hummus on one slice of bread. Top with 2 falafels.
3. Place 2 slices of tomatoes, 2 slices of cucumber, and a few slices of red onion on top of the falafel and cover with the other piece of bread.

Hints:

- You may use store bought hummus if you are pressed for time

Dinner | **DAY 21**

Vegetable Noodle Soup

Makes 4 Servings

Ingredients

For the soup:

2 tablespoons NHF extra virgin olive oil

1 yellow onion, diced

2 carrots, peeled and diced

2 stalks celery, diced

3 garlic cloves

1/2 cup whole wheat orzo, or other small pasta

1 teaspoon NHF kosher salt, or to taste

1/2 teaspoon NHF course ground black pepper, or to taste

4 cups vegetable stock

1 lemon, juiced

For the garnish:

1 small bunch Italian parsley, finely chopped

NHF lemon olive oil

Method

For the soup:

1. Place a soup pot over high heat. Once the pot is hot, add extra virgin olive oil.
2. Add the onion, carrot, and celery, and cook over high heat for 4 minutes, until the onions are soft.
3. Add the garlic and season with some of the salt and pepper.
4. Add the pasta and stir to coat with the olive oil.
5. Add the stock, and simmer for 15 minutes, until the pasta is cooked and the carrots are tender when pierced with a fork.
6. Stir in the lemon juice and add salt and pepper to taste.

For the assembly:

1. Set out 4 soup bowls. Ladle the soup into the bowls.
2. Sprinkle Italian parsley over the center of the soup and drizzle with lemon olive oil.

Continuing Your Journey: Life After the 21-Day Challenge

Congratulations! You've completed the 21-Day Challenge, and by doing so, you've made an incredible change in your life by taking charge of your health. We hope that the recipes you've prepared these past few weeks will stay in your family for generations.

But it is important that you don't stop here! Many people find the magic of a plant-based diet cumulative and feel healthier every month they continue the lifestyle. By completing the challenge, you've accomplished so much in just three weeks—imagine what you're capable of these next few years.

As I mentioned in my welcome message of this booklet, *Nature Has Flavor* is a growing community of individuals dedicated to improving their health through the plant-based lifestyle. We encourage you to join our Facebook group at **Facebook.com/ NatureHasFlavor**, where you can share your progress, discover even more recipes, and chat with other members.

Nature Has Flavor Seminars

Beyond social media, we hope to meet you in person at a *Nature Has Flavor: Become Your Own Plant-Based Chef* seminar. Through this interactive workshop, you'll see how the world's top plant-based chefs create and prepare meals, allowing you to turn your kitchen into a playground for delicious, robust creations.

Just some of the seminar's highlights include:

- A detailed presentation on the health benefits of a plant-based diet, and how proper plant-based meal preparation can help fight high cholesterol, heart disease, diabetes, and weight gain
- Speeches from some of the world's foremost plant-based experts and chefs
- Plant-based cooking demonstrations and tastings
- Hands-on cooking classes, including one-on-one interaction with professional plant-based chefs
- Detailed tips on transitioning to the plant-based lifestyle, including advice on how to incorporate a plant-based diet into your family's current routine

- Chef's secrets on how to shop for plant-based foods
- A step-by-step guide to stocking your kitchen and pantry
- An extensive Q & A session with our chefs and plant-based experts

To see seminar dates and locations, visit **Naturehasflavor.com/plant-based-seminars**.

At Home Program

Need extra help in the kitchen? Want to take your culinary skills to the next level? Through the *Nature Has Flavor At-Home Program*, our world-class chefs will teach you the secrets to making every plant-based meal savory and memorable—all from the comfort of your own kitchen.

By enrolling in the *Nature Has Flavor At-Home Program*, you will receive one-on-one training from an experienced plant-based chef in every aspect of meal preparation. **And by the end of your training, you will be ready to create a lifetime of mouthwatering plant-based meals.** You'll never be bored with healthy food again.

Traditional cooking schools do not offer specific plant-based programs, leaving plant-based food enthusiasts without a place to further their culinary skill sets. Our "At Home" program will put you on the path to plant-based culinary mastery.

How it Works

Through our *At-Home Program*, one of our world-class chefs will visit your home for 3, 5, or 7 days of instruction and information. The chef will arrive each morning to teach you how to prepare a healthy breakfast and send you on your way with a prepared lunch. At dinner, the chef will return to help you prepare your evening meal.

Along with the culinary instruction, our chefs will provide the following:

- Lifestyle tips transitioning to a plant-based diet, including tips on how to navigate social pressures inside and outside of your home
- Detailed instruction on pantry and kitchen preparation
- Menus and recipes for 3, 5, or 7 days

The chef will also accompany you to your local supermarket to gather the foods and spices you'll need for your meals.

The *Nature Has Flavor At-Home Program* is the perfect way for families and life partners to bring plant-based cooking into their household. The program is also popular among single women and men looking to prepare healthy plant-based meals on the go.

To learn more about the Nature Has Flavor At Home Program, visit **NatureHasFlavor.com/Cooking-at-Home/**.

Notes

Notes

Notes

Notes

www.ingramcontent.com/pod-product-compliance
Lightning Source LLC
Chambersburg PA
CBHW041230020526
44118CB00046B/2847